SCOTT FORESMAN · ADDISON WESLEY

Mathematics

Grade 4

Spiral Review and Test Prep Masters

PEARSON

Scott
Foresman

Editorial Offices: Glenview, Illinois • Parsippany, New Jersey • New York, New York

Sales Offices: Parsippany, New Jersey • Duluth, Georgia • Glenview, Illinois
Coppell, Texas • Ontario, California • Mesa, Arizona

Overview

Spiral Review Test Prep provides students with a continuous review of concepts presented in earlier lessons or in the previous grade. There is a one-page *Spiral Review Test Prep* for each pupil lesson with questions in multiple-choice and free-response format.

ISBN 0-328-04980-8

12 13 14 15 16 V084 09 08 07

Spiral Review and Test Prep 1-1

Circle the correct answer.

1. How many grams are there in 4 kg?

  A. 1,000   **C.** 4,000
  B. 2,000   **D.** 8,000

2. How would you describe this statement about Lana?

Lana will run 55 mi in 5 min.

  A. Certain
  B. Likely
  C. Unlikely
  D. Impossible

3. Name this polygon.

  A. Hexagon
  B. Pentagon
  C. Octagon
  D. Quadrilateral

Solve the problem by working backward.

4. Donald cut a board into two equal pieces. Then he cut 8 in. off one of the pieces. This piece is now 25 in. long. How long was the original board?

_____

Find the product.

5.   63
     $\times$ 3
     _____

6. What temperature is shown?

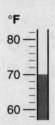

_____

Spiral Review and Test Prep 1-2

Circle the correct answer.

1. What is the value of the underlined digit in 8̲03,719?

   A. 800,000
   B. 80,000
   C. 8,000
   D. 800

2. How many ounces are in 4 lbs?

   A. 16 oz   **C.** 64 oz
   B. 32 oz   **D.** 72 oz

3. Derrick has 6 notebooks. Juan has twice as many. How many notebooks does Juan have?

   A. 8   **C.** 16
   B. 12   **D.** 18

Solve the problem by working backward.

4. Felix ate 3 energy bars on his Monday hike and 4 on his Tuesday hike. On Wednesday morning, he had 5 energy bars left. How many energy bars did Felix start with?

_____

5. Which is more, 200 mL of milk or 1 L of milk?

_____

Divide.

6. $12 \div 3 =$ _____

7. $24 \div 4 =$ _____

8. $72 \div 8 =$ _____

Name_____

Spiral Review and Test Prep 1-3

Circle the correct answer.

1. If you toss a number cube, what is the probability of tossing a 5?

A. 1 out of 3
B. 1 out of 4
C. 1 out of 5
D. 1 out of 6

2. Which number is one million more than 12,986,546?

A. 11,986,546
B. 12,986,546
C. 13,986,546
D. 120,986,546

3. At which temperature would you swim outside?

A. 5°C   **C.** 5°F
B. 30°C   **D.** 30°F

Solve the problem by working backward.

4. Mario spent $4.50 on rolls and $2.25 on milk. He had $18.00 left in his pocket. How much money did he have before he bought the rolls and milk?

_____

Add.

5.   45
       + 6
      ─────

6.   326
      + 42
      ─────

7.   451
      + 269
      ─────

Name_____

Spiral Review and Test Prep 1-4

Circle the correct answer.

1. Add.

$$30,000 + 50,000 + 200$$

A. 35,200
B. 80,200
C. 350,200
D. 800,200

2. Federico bought a box of juice for $1.29. He paid with a $5 bill. How much change did he receive?

A. $3.71   **C.** $2.71
B. $3.31   **D.** $2.31

3. How many tens are in 3,600?

A. 3   **C.** 360
B. 36   **D.** 3,600

4. $42 \div 7 =$

A. 5   **C.** 7
B. 6   **D.** 8

5. Which is more, 8 qt or 8 gal?

_____

6. Which is more, 2 L or 2 mL?

_____

Solve the problem by working backward.

7. In 2001, a player hit 73 home runs, breaking the record for the most home runs hit in one season. This was 3 more home runs than the previous record holder. What was the home run record before it was broken in 2001?

_____

Spiral Review and Test Prep 1-5

Circle the correct answer.

1. The letters *A, B, E, C, I, O,* and *F* are written on slips of paper and placed inside a bag. What is the probability of pulling out a slip of paper that has a vowel written on it?

   A. 1 out of 7
   B. 2 out of 5
   C. 4 out of 7
   D. 5 out of 7

2. Sue has 11 books, Bill has 7 books, and Benito has 12 books. How many books are there altogether?

   A. 27   **C.** 31
   B. 30   **D.** 127

3. What is another way to write "5 out of 8"?

   A. $\frac{5}{8}$ **C.** 5–8
   B. 5:8   **D.** 5, 8

4. Look for a pattern. Write the next three numbers.

18,256 18,356 18,456

_____

_____

How many more days begin with the letter *S* than the letter *M*?

5. Tell what you know in your own words.

_____

_____

_____

6. Solve the problem.

_____

_____

_____

_____

_____

Spiral Review and Test Prep 1-6

Circle the correct answer.

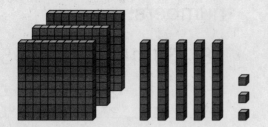

1. How would you write this number in standard form?

  A. 235   **C.** 335

  B. 253   **D.** 353

2. Find 2×7.

  A. 12   **C.** 16

  B. 14   **D.** 18

3. Which number completes the number sentence?

$$18 = \underline{\hspace{1cm}} + (4 + 4)$$

  A. 4   **C.** 10

  B. 8   **D.** 16

4. Order the numbers from least to greatest.

  27,054   27,256

  26,966   27,276

_____

Solve the problem by working backward.

5. Monday afternoon Tomasino found 14 trading cards in his drawer and bought 5 cards from Joel. Tomasino now has 51 cards. How many did he have Monday morning?

_____

6. Which is less, 9 qt of water or 2 gal of water?

_____

7. Which is heavier, a 2 kg or a 1,000 g watermelon?

_____

Name_____

Spiral Review and Test Prep 1-7

Circle the correct answer.
Solve the problem by
working backward.

1. Aurelio spent $3.80 on
   lunch and $7.55 on
   dinner. At the end of the
   day, he had $15.50 in
   his wallet. How much
   money did he start the
   day with?

   A. $26.85 C. $19.30
   B. $23.05 D. $11.35

2. How would you write
   $6\frac{3}{10}$ as a decimal?

   A. 0.63   C. 6.3
   B. 6.03   D. 63.10

3. Which number is
   657,782 rounded to the
   nearest 10,000?

   A. 650,000 C. 660,000
   B. 656,000 D. 665,000

Spinner Game

Player A scores a point if
the spinner lands on an
even number.

Player B scores a point if
the spinner lands on an
odd number.

4. Would this be a fair
   game using this
   spinner? Why?

   _____

   _____

   _____

   _____

   _____

   _____

Spiral Review and Test Prep 1-8

Circle the correct answer.

1. How many 1,000s equal 100,000?

   A. 10   C. 1,000
   B. 100   D. 10,000

2. Marco took a walk after breakfast, lunch, and dinner. He walked 2 mi after lunch and 4 mi after dinner. He walked a total of 14 mi. How many miles did he walk after breakfast?

   A. 5   C. 7
   B. 6   D. 8

3. Find $25 \div x = 5$.

   A. 3   C. 15
   B. 5   D. 75

4. A box holds 100 pencils. How many pencils are in 70 boxes?

   A. 700   C. 70,000
   B. 7,000   D. 700,000

5. A whale shark can grow to be 50 ft long. How long would 80 whale sharks placed end-to-end be?

   _____

6. Compare. Use <, >, or =.

   4,512 ____ 4,521

Choose the better estimate for each activity.

7. snow skiing

   26°F or 76°F _____

8. skate boarding

   13°F or 30°C _____

9. swimming

   85°F or 80°C _____

10. Round 639,258 to the nearest hundred thousand.

    _____

Spiral Review and Test Prep 1-9

Circle the correct answer.

Use the spinner for 1–2.

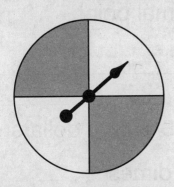

1. What is the probability of the spinner landing on a shaded section?

A. 1 out of 8
B. 3 out of 8
C. 2 out of 4
D. 4 out of 4

2. Which word best describes the probability of the spinner landing on an odd-numbered section?

A. Certain
B. Possible
C. Impossible
D. Unlikely

A bucket contains 23 worms for fishing. Wanda added 17 more worms. How many worms does the bucket contain now?

Dana's Work

23 + 17 = 40 worms

There are now 40 worms in

the bucket.

3. Name the strategy Dana used to solve the problem.

_____

_____

A jar holds 50 marbles. How many marbles are in

4. 100 jars?

_____

5. 500 jars?

_____

Spiral Review and Test Prep 1-10

Circle the correct answer.

1. How many pints are in 6 c?

    A. 1 pt   **C.** 3 pt
    B. 2 pt   **D.** 4 pt

2.

What is the time?

    A. 12:35   **C.** 7:00
    B. 1:35   **D.** 7:05

Solve the problem by working backward.

3. Vaughn cut a piece of floor tile in half. He then cut 2 cm off one of the pieces. The piece is now 10 cm long. How long was the original piece of floor tile?

    A. 12 cm   **C.** 24 cm
    B. 20 cm   **D.** 28 cm

4. Write 4 dollars, 7 dimes, and 5 pennies with a dollar sign and a decimal point.

_____

5. $5.18 = ____ dollars +

____ dimes + ____ pennies

5.18 = ____ ones +

____ tenth + ____ hundredths

6. $6.23 = ____ dollars +

____ pennies

6.23 = ____ ones +

____ hundredths

7. Write 2 lb 4 oz in ounces.

_____

Name_____

Spiral Review and Test Prep 1-11

Circle the correct answer.

1. Count the money. What is the amount?

4 dimes

A. $4.00   C. $0.04
B. $0.40   D. $0.004

2. Which number is 56,247 rounded to the nearest hundred?

A. 56,200   C. 56,300
B. 56,250   D. 56,350

3. Subtract.

   300
 − 192

A. 88
B. 108
C. 118
D. 208

4. Count the money. What is the amount?

6 dollars, 2 quarters, 3 nickels

A. $6.50   C. $6.65
B. $6.55   D. $6.75

Solve the problem by working backward.

5. Tammy arrived at work at 9:30. Her train ride lasted 35 min and her bus ride took 55 min. At what time did she leave the house?

_____

_____

Write each temperature using °F.

6.

_____

7.

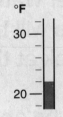

_____

Name_____

Spiral Review and Test Prep 1-12

Circle the correct answer.

1. If you tossed a number cube, what is the probability you would toss an 8?

A. 0 in 6   **C.** 2 in 4
B. 1 in 2   **D.** 4 in 8

2. Each side of a square is 9 ft long. What is the perimeter of the square?

A. 9 ft   **C.** 36 ft
B. 18 ft   **D.** 45 ft

3. Which of the following events are possible?

A. Dogs will write sentences.
B. Airplanes will be flown under water.
C. Telescopes will be used to look at the moon.
D. Books will be able to play baseball.

List the coins and bills you would give as change for the purchase.

4. Cost: $10.50

_____

_____

_____

Solve the problem by working backward.

5. Franny added more plants to her garden. She planted 11 tomato plants and 4 green pepper plants. She now has 45 plants in her garden. How many plants were in her garden before she added more?

_____

Spiral Review and Test Prep 1-13

Circle the correct answer.

1. Clara built a toy tower with blocks. She added blocks to increase the height by 7 in. Then she placed a 3-inch-tall block at the top. The tower was now 32 inches tall. How tall was the original tower?

   A. 12 in.   **C.** 32 in.
   B. 22 in.   **D.** 42 in.

2. How many quarts are in 4 gal?

   A. 4   **C.** 20
   B. 16   **D.** 24

3. $\angle ABC$ is 60°. What type of angle is $\angle ABC$?

   A. Acute   **C.** Obtuse
   B. Right   **D.** Straight

4. How many mL are in 3 L?

   A. 30   **C.** 3,000
   B. 300   **D.** 30,000

Write the word name and decimal for each shaded part.

5.

_____

_____

6.

_____

_____

7. Shade the grid to show the decimal 0.59.

Spiral Review and Test Prep 1-14

Circle the correct answer.

1. There are 10 names in a hat. There are 4 girls' names and the rest are boys' names. What is the probability of drawing a girl's name from the hat?

   A. 1 out of 10
   B. 2 out of 10
   C. 4 out of 10
   D. 6 out of 10

2. Which of these words best describes the temperature 98°F?

   A. Cold   **C.** Warm
   B. Cool   **D.** Hot

3. Leon bought a guitar that cost $137.67. He gave the clerk a $100 bill and a $50 bill. How much change should he get back?

   A. $0.23   **C.** $12.33
   B. $1.23   **D.** $23.30

Solve the problem by working backward.

4. On Tuesday, Ramon's hat collection increased when he got 2 hats as a gift. Later, he purchased another hat. He now has 43 hats. How many hats were in his collection before Tuesday?

_____

Clayton earns 3 stickers each night for going to bed on time. How many nights will it take him to earn 33 stickers?

Amy's Work

30 ÷ 3 = 10
Clayton will have to go to bed on time for 10 nights.

5. Did Amy's work match the information in the problem?

_____

Name_____

Spiral Review and Test Prep 2-1

Circle the correct answer.

1. Multiply.

$30 \times 100 =$

- **A.** 300
- **B.** 3,000
- **C.** 30,000
- **D.** 300,000

2. Count the money:
3 dollars, 2 quarters,
3 dimes.

- **A.** $3.80
- **C.** $4.80
- **B.** $3.95
- **D.** $5.00

3. Subtract.

$28 - 13 =$

- **A.** 12
- **C.** 14
- **B.** 13
- **D.** 15

4. Which is the word name for the decimal 0.43?

- **A.** 43 tenths
- **B.** 43 hundredths
- **C.** 43 thousandths
- **D.** 43 ones

5. Elaine bought a CD that cost $13.67. She gave the clerk a $20.00 bill. How much change should she get back?

_____

6. Tammi has 7 toy trains. Her father gave her 2 toy trains for her birthday. How many toy trains does Tammi have now?

Hal found the answer:
$7 + 2 = 9$.

Name the strategy Hal used to solve the problem.

_____

Add.

7. $45 + 32 =$ _____

8. $23 + 61 =$ _____

9. $80 + 19 =$ _____

Spiral Review and Test Prep 2-2

Circle the correct answer.

1. Add. Use mental math.

$90 + 500$

A. 140   **C.** 600

B. 590   **D.** 950

2. Subtract.

$$5.7$$
$$-\ 2.3$$

A. 2.4   **C.** 3.4

B. 2.7   **D.** 3.7

3. Round 346,721 to the nearest thousand.

A. 340,000

B. 346,000

C. 347,000

D. 350,000

4. Estimate the product of 72×9.

A. 81   **C.** 600

B. 270   **D.** 720

5. Order the numbers from greatest to least.

345,002   345,000

354,200   354,020

_____

_____

6. Everett found 19 rocks. He gave 7 of them to the school's rock collection. Then Everett found 3 more rocks. How many rocks does he have now?

_____

7. Jill reads 4 chapters of her book every day. If she did this for 10 days, how many chapters did she read in all? Solve the problem. Write the answer in a complete sentence.

_____

_____

Spiral Review and Test Prep 2-3

Circle the correct answer.

1. What is the standard form of five million, two hundred seventy thousand, six hundred nine?

   A. 52,769
   B. 5,200,769
   C. 5,207,609
   D. 5,270,609

2. Subtract. Use mental math.

   $168 - 42$

   A. 126   C. 136
   B. 128   D. 138

3. Each piggy bank holds 1,000 coins. How many coins are there in 40 piggy banks?

   A. 4,000
   B. 40,000
   C. 400,000
   D. 4,000,000

4. Destiny has 9 more stickers than Quincy. Quincy has 11 stickers. How many stickers does Destiny have?

   _____

5. There are 58 fourth graders at Stephen's school. Ten of these students are at the school spelling bee. The others watched the school play. How many fourth graders watched the play?

   _____

6. It takes Hunter 3 min to run around the track. How many minutes will it take him to run around the track 4 times?

   _____

Name_____

Spiral Review and Test Prep 2-4

Circle the correct answer.

Batter	Hits
A	153
B	109
C	78
D	123

1. Round 846,099 to the nearest hundred thousand.

   A. 800,000
   B. 840,000
   C. 850,000
   D. 900,000

4. About how many hits did Batter A and Batter B have altogether?

_____

2. Which of the following shows $5.39 with the fewest bills and coins?

   A. 5 dollars, 3 dimes, 9 pennies
   B. 1 five-dollar bill, 1 quarter, 1 dime, 4 pennies
   C. 1 five-dollar bill, 3 dimes, 1 nickel, 4 pennies
   D. 1 five-dollar bill, 3 dimes, 9 pennies

5. About how many more hits did Batter D have than Batter C?

_____

6. At a golf tournament, Wendi scored a 79 on her first round, 82 on her second round, and 77 on her third round. What was Wendi's total score?

_____

3. Add.

$$\begin{array}{r} 321 \\ +\ 472 \\ \hline \end{array}$$

   A. 693
   B. 773
   C. 793
   D. 803

Name_____

Spiral Review and Test Prep 2-5

Circle the correct answer.

1. Hailey bought a hat for $15.44. She paid with a $20.00 bill. How much change should she receive?

   A. $4.54   **C.** $4.66
   B. $4.56   **D.** $5.56

2. Which is the value of the underlined digit?

6<u>5</u>2,108

   A. 500   **C.** 50,000
   B. 5,000 **D.** 500,000

3. Estimate the sum. Then tell whether your estimate is an overestimate or an underestimate.

743 + 235

   A. 900; underestimate
   B. 900; overestimate
   C. 1,000; underestimate
   D. 1,000; overestimate

4. Margo saw 26 ducks at the park in the morning. She went home for lunch. Margo went back to the park in the afternoon and saw 13 more ducks. How many ducks did Margo see altogether?

_____

5. Miles estimated 843 + 135 by adding 800 + 100. Is this an overestimate or an underestimate?

_____

Subtract.

6. 298 − 71 = _____

7. 767 − 214 = _____

Spiral Review and Test Prep 2-6

Circle the correct answer.

1. Add. Use mental math.

27 + 62

A. 79   C. 97
B. 89   D. 99

2. Which numbers come next in the pattern?

3,455   3,465   3,475

A. 3,485   C. 3,505
B. 3,495   D. 3,685

3. $36.25 + $12.94

A. $37.98   C. $49.19
B. $45.00   D. $50.00

4. There are 12 in. in 1 ft. How many inches are in 3 ft?

A. 12 in.   C. 30 in.
B. 24 in.   D. 36 in.

The students at Tayshaun's school were surveyed about their favorite color.

Color	Votes
Blue	216
Red	378
Green	192
Yellow	139

5. Altogether, how many students like green and yellow?

_____

6. Mickey added 345 + 237 and got 572. Does Mickey have the right answer? Explain.

_____

_____

_____

_____

7. Compare. Write > or < for the ____.

722,982 ____ 722,892

Name_____

Spiral Review and Test Prep 2-7

Circle the correct answer.

1. Add

```
  2,145
    410
  4,899
+ 1,438
```

A. 8,453   **C.** 8,882
B. 8,763   **D.** 8,892

2. Round 12,389,004 to the nearest hundred thousand.

A. 12,000,000
B. 12,300,000
C. 12,390,000
D. 12,400,000

3. If there are 10,000 bees in 1 hive, how many bees are in 5 hives?

A. 5,000
B. 50,000
C. 500,000
D. 5,000,000

4. Jasmine handed out flyers for a charity event. She started with 775 flyers and ended with 211. How many flyers did Jasmine hand out? Draw a picture to help you solve the problem.

_____

Multiply.

5. 12 × 4

_____

6. 20 × 10

_____

Spiral Review and Test Prep 2-8

Circle the correct answer.

1. Which is the standard form of 3 ten thousands + 2 thousands + 4 hundreds + 8 ones?

   A. 32,408   C. 30,248
   B. 32,480   D. 30,240

2. $5.82   A. $0.33
   −   3.49   B. $1.33
                  C. $1.83
                  D. $2.33

3. Divide.

   144 ÷ 12

   A. 10   C. 12
   B. 11   D. 13

4. Compare.

   4,038 _____ 4,048

   A. <   C. =
   B. >   D. ÷

Lilith brought 20 cans to the food drive. Marcus brought 7 cans to the food drive. If Paulina brought 8 more cans than Lilith and Marcus combined, how many cans did Paulina bring?

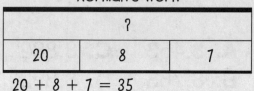

Norman's Work

?		
20	8	7

20 + 8 + 7 = 35

So, Paulina brought 35 cans to the food drive.

5. Did Norman answer the right question? Is he correct?

   _____

Subtract.

6. 803 − 79

   _____

7. $30.00 − $16.48

   _____

Spiral Review and Test Prep 2-9

Circle the correct answer.

1. To what place is the number 12,340,000 rounded?

   A. Tens
   B. Hundreds
   C. Thousands
   D. Ten thousands

2. Multiply.

   $\begin{array}{r} 71 \\ \times\ 12 \\ \hline \end{array}$

   A. 710
   B. 781
   C. 840
   D. 852

3. Divide.

   $100 \div 20$

   A. 4
   B. 5
   C. 6
   D. 7

4. Add. Which method did you use?

   $300 + 201$

   A. 321; mental math
   B. 501; mental math
   C. 511; paper and pencil
   D. 511; calculator

5. Tell how to make $13.82 with the fewest bills and coins.

   _____

   _____

   _____

   _____

6. The computer factory is making 3 shipments to stores. Each shipment has 100 computers. How many computers are being shipped to stores? Show the main idea of the problem.

Spiral Review and Test Prep 2-10

Circle the correct answer.

1. Add.
$$\begin{array}{r} 234 \\ 36 \\ +\ 114 \\ \hline \end{array}$$

A. 384   **C.** 508
B. 414   **D.** 708

2. Look for a pattern. Fill in the missing numbers.

10, 15, 20, ___, ___, ___

A. 22, 24, 26
B. 25, 30, 35
C. 27, 32, 37
D. 30, 40, 50

3. If there are 100 batteries in a box, how many batteries are in 80 boxes?

A. 800   **C.** 8,000
B. 1,800   **D.** 80,000

4. Look for a pattern. Draw the next two shapes.

5. Gabe wants to collect 12 box tops so he can get a free CD. If Gabe has 4 box tops saved already, how many more does he need? Write the answer and name a strategy you can use to solve this problem.

_____

6. Victoria spent $21.45. She paid the cashier with a $20 bill and a $10 bill. How much change should Victoria get?

_____

Name_____

Spiral Review and Test Prep 2-11

Circle the correct answer.

1. Subtract.

138 − 57

A. 195   **C.** 91
B. 115   **D.** 81

2. Which is a number expression for $34 increased by $11?

A. $34 + $11
B. $34 − $11
C. $34 × $11
D. $34 ÷ $11

3. Which of the following can round to 350,000?

A. 357,233
B. 355,000
C. 354,321
D. 344,321

4. Divide.

888 ÷ 8

A. 8   **C.** 88
B. 11   **D.** 111

Allan counted the number of cars parked on 4 streets. On Oak Street, there were 42 cars. On Elm Road, there were 71 cars. On Maple Drive, there were 38 cars. If Allan counted a total of 194 cars, how many cars were parked on Pine Boulevard?

Jasmine's Work

194			
71	42	38	?

71 + 42 + 38 = 151
194 − 151 = 53

So, 53 cars were parked on Pine Boulevard.

5. Is her answer correct? Explain.

_____

_____

6. Which is more, 6 dimes and 1 penny or 5 dimes and 13 pennies?

_____

_____

Spiral Review and Test Prep 2-12

Circle the correct answer.

1. Subtract. Use mental math.

678 − 482

A. 96   **C.** 196
B. 186   **D.** 206

2. Kate has 9 drawings and Mary has 16. How many drawings do they have altogether?

To solve this, Peter wrote: 9 + 16 = 25.

What strategy did Peter use to solve this problem?

A. Write an equation
B. Make an organized list
C. Draw a picture
D. Make a table

3. Add.

   839
+ 547

A. 1,199
B. 1,289
C. 1,376
D. 1,386

Write a number expression that matches the words. Then, find its value.

4. Pia had a $20 bill. She spent $7 and then earned $9. How much does she have?

_____

5. How could you make $27.31 with exactly 4 bills and 3 coins?

_____

_____

_____

6. Write the word form of 3,484,239.

_____

_____

_____

_____

Spiral Review and Test Prep 2-13

Circle the correct answer.

1. Evaluate $z - 4$ for $z = 17$.

   A. 4   **C.** 11
   B. 7   **D.** 13

2. Which number is greater than 3,429?

   A. 3,329   **C.** 3,429
   B. 3,419   **D.** 3,430

3. Kevin cut an apple into 5 pieces. Then he cut each piece in half. He ate 2 pieces. How many pieces are left?

   A. 3   **C.** 7
   B. 5   **D.** 8

4. There are 16 oz in 1 lb. How many ounces are in 8 lb?

   A. 80 oz   **C.** 160 oz
   B. 128 oz   **D.** 172 oz

5. Name 78,000 in two different ways.

   _____

   _____

   _____

The bicycle shop offers 2 different kinds of bicycles: road or mountain. The shop also offers 3 different colors: green, blue, and silver. How many different combinations of bicycles can the shop sell?

Caleb	
road–green	mountain–green
road–blue	mountain–blue
road–silver	mountain–silver
6 bicycles	

6. Name the strategy Caleb used to solve the problem.

   _____

   _____

Spiral Review and Test Prep 2-14

Circle the correct answer.

1. Solve the equation $t - 5 = 12$.

A. 5	**C.** 12
B. 7	**D.** 17

2. How many 100s equal 100,000?

A. 10	**C.** 1,000
B. 100	**D.** 10,000

3. Ezra studies for 2 hrs each day. How many hours does he study in 5 days?

A. 2	**C.** 10
B. 5	**D.** 20

4. Marvin purchased sports equipment for $83.21. He paid with five $20 bills. How much change should he receive?

A. $15.71	**C.** $17.71
B. $16.79	**D.** $17.79

Samantha enjoys collecting baseball cards. She keeps her cards in three places: an album, a box, and a display case. How many cards does Samantha have?

Album	🔵 🔵 🔵 🔵 🔵 🔵 🔵 🔵
Box	🔵 🔵 🔵 🔵 🔵 🔵
Display Case	🔵 🔵 🔵 🔵 🔵 🔵

Each 🔵 = 20 cards.

Kenneth's Work

$$160 + 120 + 110 = 395$$

So, Samantha has 395 baseball cards.

5. Is Kenneth's answer reasonable?

_____

_____

Solve the equation.

6. $b + 32 = 37$

_____

Spiral Review and Test Prep 3-1

Circle the correct answer.

River	Length (in miles)
Nile	4,160
Amazon	4,000
Chang	3,964

1. Which of the following is greater than 3,476,008?

   A. 3,476,009
   B. 3,467,009
   C. 3,467,008
   D. 3,460,708

2. Subtract. Use mental math.

   $174 - 28$

   A. 136   **C.** 146
   B. 138   **D.** 148

3. Count the money.

   6 dollars, 3 quarters, 4 dimes, 8 pennies

   A. $6.75   **C.** $7.13
   B. $6.83   **D.** $7.23

4. $5.73 + $3.65

   A. $8.38   **C.** $9.38
   B. $8.88   **D.** $9.88

5. How much longer is the Nile than the Chang?

_____

6. A rug store has two rooms. There are 1,358 rugs in the first room and 1,140 rugs in the second room. Round to the nearest hundred to estimate how many rugs are in the store.

_____

_____

7. Look for a pattern and write the missing numbers.

   1, 5, 7, 11, 13, 17, 19,

   _____, _____, _____

Spiral Review and Test Prep 3-2

Circle the correct answer.

Subtract. Use mental math.

1. 432 − 28

    A. 396   **C.** 400

    B. 398   **D.** 404

2. Round 1,326 to the nearest hundred.

    A. 1,000   **C.** 1,400

    B. 1,300   **D.** 2,000

3. Which addition expression can be used to find 4 × 7?

    A. 7 + 7

    B. 7 + 7 + 7

    C. 7 + 7 + 7 + 7

    D. 7 + 7 + 7 + 7 + 7

4.   4,567   **A.** 7,980
    + 3,423   **B.** 7,990
                  C. 7,999
                  D. 8,090

5. Thomas begins the day with $15. He buys lunch for $4 and earns $11 mowing a lawn. How much money does he have now? Write a number expression and then evaluate it.

_____

_____

6. Find 40 divided by 5.

_____

Add. Use mental math.

7. 256 + 27

_____

8. Write a multiplication sentence for the addition sentence.

    6 + 6 + 6 + 6 + 6 + 6 + 6 + 6 = 48

_____

Name_____

Spiral Review and Test Prep 3-3

Circle the correct answer.

1.   8
   $\times\ 1$

   A. 1
   B. 8
   C. 9
   D. 18

2. Evaluate the expression for $y = 12$.

   $10 + y =$

   A. 12   **C.** 22
   B. 13   **D.** 23

3. Solve the equation.

   $20 + k = 34$

   A. $k = 11$ **C.** $k = 13$
   B. $k = 12$ **D.** $k = 14$

4. $34.78
   $+\quad 23.20$

   A. $58.98
   B. $57.98
   C. $57.88
   D. $57.78

5. Look for a pattern. Tell the missing numbers.

   8, 16, 24, 32, _____,

   _____, _____

6. A bucket holds 100 golf balls. How many golf balls are in 300 buckets?

   _____

7. Find $\frac{1}{5}$ of 35.

   _____

8. Tell how you would give change from a $20.00 bill for a purchase of $14.62. List the bills and coins you would use and give the amount with a dollar sign and decimal point.

   _____

   _____

   _____

Spiral Review and Test Prep 3-4

Circle the correct answer.

1. 345
     $+\ 169$

   A. 614
   B. 534
   C. 524
   D. 514

2. Use breaking apart to find the product.

   6×9

   A. 56   **C.** 52
   B. 54   **D.** 48

3. Divide.

   $72 \div 9$

   A. 9   **C.** 7
   B. 8   **D.** 6

4. Evaluate the expression for $x = 15$.

   $x + 40 =$

   A. 15   **C.** 45
   B. 35   **D.** 55

5. Write a number expression for this phrase.

   172 is how much more than 88?

   _____

6. Peter has $10.00. He buys a notebook for $2.95 and a package of pencils for $1.19. How much money does he have left?

   _____

7. Pearl is collecting stamps from the local sandwich shop. For every 6 stamps she collects, Pearl receives a free sandwich. How many stamps will Pearl need to collect to receive 4 free sandwiches?

   _____

Name_____

Spiral Review and Test Prep 3-5

Circle the correct answer.

1. 10 × 11

   A. 100   **C.** 1,011
   B. 110   **D.** 1,100

2. Which expression can be used to find 8 × 4?

   A. 8 + 4 + 2
   B. 8 × 4 + 2
   C. (8 × 2) + (8 × 2)
   D. (8 × 2) + (8 × 4)

3. Round 21,426 to the nearest thousand.

   A. 21,000   **C.** 21,500
   B. 21,400   **D.** 22,000

4. Tamara served 5 dozen biscuits at a picnic. How many biscuits did she serve?

   A. 50   **C.** 62
   B. 60   **D.** 70

5. Look for a pattern and write the missing numbers.

   2, 9, 16, 23, 30, 37,

   _____, _____, _____

6. $213.35
           46.25
   +   0.49
   _____

7. Name the solid figure this object looks like.

_____

Evaluate each expression for $z = 21$.

8. $z + 206$ _____

9. $32 - z$ _____

Spiral Review and Test Prep 3-6

Circle the correct answer.

1. Solve the equation.

$43 - d = 38$

A. $d = 3$ **C.** $d = 5$
B. $d = 4$ **D.** $d = 6$

2.
$$\begin{array}{r} 7{,}209 \\ -\ 6{,}771 \\ \hline \end{array}$$
A. 456
B. 452
C. 448
D. 438

3. Which of the following expressions can be used to find 5×12?

A. $(2 \times 12) + (3 \times 12)$
B. $(5 \times 12) + (1 \times 12)$
C. $(2 \times 12) + (4 \times 12)$
D. $(3 \times 12) + (1 \times 12)$

4.
$$\begin{array}{r} 10{,}323 \\ +\ 3{,}428 \\ \hline \end{array}$$
A. 13,741
B. 13,751
C. 13,841
D. 13,851

Complete the table to solve the problem. Write the answer in a complete sentence.

5. Georgia is making baskets. She made 3 baskets the first day and 5 baskets each day after that. How many baskets did Georgia make in 5 days?

Days	1	2	3	4	5
Baskets	3	8	13		

_____

_____

_____

Write a number expression and then evaluate it.

6. Ray has 15 bean plants. He plants them in 3 equal rows. How many plants are in each row?

_____

Name_____

Spiral Review and Test Prep 3-7

Circle the correct answer.

1. A bag of 12 fruit snacks is divided equally among 3 friends. Which expression can be used to find the number of snacks each person received?

    A. 4×12
    B. $12 \div 3$
    C. 2×6
    D. $12 \div 4$

2. Subtract.

    $347 - 38$

    A. 319   **C.** 309
    B. 318   **D.** 308

3. Evaluate the expression for $g = 5$.

    $50 + g$

    A. 50   **C.** 60
    B. 55   **D.** 65

Write an expression and then evaluate it.

4. Greenville School has 162 band members. During the year, 19 students join the band. How many students are in the band now?

_____

_____

_____

Estimate the sum. Then tell whether your estimate is an overestimate or an underestimate.

5. $43 + 32$ _____

_____

6. Add.

      6.39
    $+\ 2.83$

Spiral Review and Test Prep 3-8

Circle the correct answer.

1. How many inches are in 6 feet?

    A. 6 in.   **C.** 36 in.

    B. 12 in.   **D.** 72 in.

Choose the number expression that matches the words.

2. Janine has 9 pet fish. She gave her brother 3 of the fish, and her mother gave Janine 5 new fish. How many fish does Janine have now?

    A. $9 + 3 - 5$

    B. $9 + 3 + 5$

    C. $9 - 3 + 5$

    D. $9 - 3 - 5$

3. Estimate the sum.

    $3{,}402 + 2{,}199$

    A. 5,100   **C.** 5,700

    B. 5,600   **D.** 6,000

4. Write the fact family for 6, 4, and 24.

_____

_____

_____

_____

5. What multiplication fact could be used to help you find $27 \div 3$?

_____

6. Look for a pattern. Draw the next two shapes.

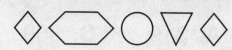

7.   7
  $\times\ 8$
  ‾‾‾‾

Name_____

Spiral Review and Test Prep 3-9

Circle the correct answer.

	Store A	Store B
CDs	12,743	10,825
Books	14,434	12,685

1. In a science class, 36 students are placed into 4 equal groups. How many students are in each group?

   A. 12   **C.** 4
   B. 9   **D.** 3

2. Neil has $12.56. Later that day he finds a $5.00 bill in his coat pocket. He spends $1.46 at the store. Which expression can be used to find out how much money Neil has now?

   A. $12.56 − $5.00 + $1.46
   B. $12.56 + $5.00 − $1.46
   C. $12.56 − $5.00 − $1.46
   D. $12.56 + $5.00 + $1.46

3. How many books are there altogether in the two stores?

   _____

4. How many more CDs are there in Store A than in Store B?

   _____

5. Look for a pattern and write the missing numbers.

   10, 22, 34, 46, 58, _____,

   _____, _____

6. Jakki worked 3 hrs each day for 12 days. How many hours did Jakki work?

   _____

Spiral Review and Test Prep 3-10

Circle the correct answer.

1. $8 \div 1$

  A. 0   **C.** 8

  B. 1   **D.** 9

2. Which expression CANNOT be used to evaluate $248 + 67$?

  A. $(248 + 60) + 7$
  B. $(248 + 52) + 15$
  C. $(248 + 70) - 3$
  D. $(248 + 50) + 7$

3. Solve the equation.

  $103 - q = 97$

  A. $q = 6$ **C.** $q = 4$
  B. $q = 5$ **D.** $q = 3$

4. There are 24 teams in the league. The league is divided into 4 divisions. How many teams are in each division?

  A. 4   **C.** 8
  B. 6   **D.** 12

Compare. Use $>$, $<$, or $=$ for _____.

5. $0 \div 1$ _____ $0 \div 7$

6. Sandra has 153 comic books. She sells 24 old comics at a garage sale and uses the money to buy 6 new comic books. How many comic books does Sandra have now? Write a number expression and then evaluate it.

_____

_____

7.   2,612
          16,867
     $+$ 42,005

Describe the statement as certain, likely, unlikely, or impossible.

8. A dog will sing.

_____

Name_____

Spiral Review and Test Prep 3-11

Circle the correct answer.

1. An egg carton holds 24 eggs in 3 rows. How many eggs are in each row?

   A. 8   **C.** 10

   B. 9   **D.** 12

2. Evaluate the expression for $x = 3$.

   $x + 7$

   A. 3   **C.** 9

   B. 7   **D.** 10

3. Solve the equation.

   $32 + n = 32$

   A. $n = 0$ **C.** $n = 3$

   B. $n = 2$ **D.** $n = 32$

4. $0 \div 18$

   A. 18   **C.** 1

   B. 10   **D.** 0

5. Ellen parked her car in a lot that cost $3 per hour. She parked for 4 hours. How much did it cost for Ellen to park her car? Write a number expression and then evaluate it.

_____

6.   1,678
        1,918
  + 23,529
_____

Write a multiplication or division story for the number fact.

7. 8×3

_____

_____

_____

_____

_____

Name_____

Spiral Review and Test Prep 3-12

Circle the correct answer.

1. Subtract. Use mental math.

   700 − 200

   A. 500   **C.** 420
   B. 450   **D.** 400

2. Which of the following computation methods would be easiest for 2,000 + 1,000?

   A. Paper and pencil
   B. Calculator
   C. Computer
   D. Mental math

3. 72×4

   A. 248   **C.** 360
   B. 288   **D.** 388

Write and answer the hidden question. Then solve the problem. Write your answer in a complete sentence.

4. A small bag holds 2 books. Six large bags hold 30 books. How many more books can you carry in 6 large bags than in 6 small bags?

   _____

   _____

   _____

   _____

   _____

5. Look for a pattern and write the missing numbers.

   81, 101, 121, 141, 161,

   _____, _____, _____

Name_____

Spiral Review and Test Prep 3-13

Circle the correct answer.

1. Evaluate the expression for $d = 3$.

   $4d + 12$

   A. 24   **C.** 22

   B. 23   **D.** 20

2. Round 32,437 to the nearest thousand.

   A. 33,000   **C.** 32,400

   B. 32,500   **D.** 32,000

3. Which of the following expressions can be used to find 5×7?

   A. $(2 \times 7) + (4 \times 7)$

   B. $7 + 7 + 7 + 7$

   C. $(2 \times 7) + (3 \times 7)$

   D. $7 + 7 + 7 + 7 + 7 + 7$

4. Add. Use mental math.

   $234 + 58$

   A. 282   **C.** 302

   B. 292   **D.** 312

5. A mother bird has 6 worms. She finds 7 more worms. Then she feeds 8 of the worms to her babies. How many worms does the mother bird have left? Write a number expression and then evaluate it.

   _____

6. Franklyn bought 6 tomatoes, some green peppers, and twice as many cucumbers as green peppers. The total number of vegetables, including g green peppers, is $6 + g + 2g$. Find the total number of vegetables Franklyn bought if he bought 5 green peppers.

   _____

Spiral Review and Test Prep 3-14

Circle the correct answer.

1. Evaluate the expression for $a = 6$.

$3a - 12$

A. 4   **C.** 10
B. 6   **D.** 12

2. $256.88   **A.** $601.01
   +   345.13   **B.** $602.01
               C. $603.11
               D. $612.01

3. If you know that $5 \times d = 35$, which of the following facts is NOT true?

A. $d \times 5 = 35$
B. $35 \div 7 = d$
C. $35 \div d = 5$
D. $d = 7$

4. Which number is less than 8,619?

A. 8,916   **C.** 8,620
B. 8,691   **D.** 8,196

5. Complete the table. Write the rule.

In	3	4	5	6	k
Out	9	12		18	

_____

_____

6. Look for a pattern and write the missing numbers.

7, 19, 31, 43, 55, _____,

_____, _____

7. $9 \times 7 =$ _____

8. $9 \times 9 =$ _____

9. Complete the table. Write the rule.

In	12	16	20	4	n
Out	3		5		

_____

_____

Spiral Review and Test Prep 3-15

Circle the correct answer.

1. Solve the equation by testing these values for x: 8, 12, 16, and 24.

   $x \div 6 = 4$

   A. $x = 8$ C. $x = 16$
   B. $x = 12$ D. $x = 24$

2. Subtract.

   $$\begin{array}{r} \$84.00 \\ -\ 23.78 \\ \hline \end{array}$$

   A. $60.22
   B. $60.32
   C. $61.22
   D. $61.33

3. Which of the following is the number expression for this phrase?

   11 coats, but 8 more hats

   A. $11 - 8$ C. 11×8
   B. $10 + 8$ D. $11 + 8$

4.
   $$\begin{array}{r} 5{,}615 \\ 17{,}432 \\ +\ 63{,}456 \\ \hline \end{array}$$

5. Solve the equation by testing these values for m: 3, 5, 7, and 9.

   $8m = 56$

   _____

   _____

   _____

   _____

   _____

The Eiffel Tower in Paris is 986 ft tall and was the tallest structure in the world in 1889. It remained the tallest structure in the world until 1930, when the Empire State Building in New York City was finished. The Empire State Building is 1,250 ft tall.

6. For how long was the Eiffel Tower the tallest structure in the world?

   _____

Spiral Review and Test Prep 4-1

Circle the correct answer.

1. Add.

$23.42
+ 18.95

    A. $40.37
    B. $42.17
    C. $42.37
    D. $43.27

2. If there are 100 pages in each book, how many pages are in 50 books?

    A. 500   **C.** 50,000
    B. 5,000   **D.** 500,000

3.

What time is shown on the clock?

    A. 10:25   **C.** 5:11
    B. 9:22   **D.** 4:48

Write and answer the hidden question. Then solve the problem.

4. Bobby has 4 sheets of stickers with 9 stickers on each sheet. If the stickers are split evenly between 3 people, how many stickers will each person get?

_____

_____

_____

_____

Compare. Use >, <, or = for each _____.

5. $7 \div 7$ _____ $1 \div 1$

6. $0 \div 4$ _____ $9 \div 1$

Evaluate the expression for $t = 20$.

7. $t \div 5$ _____

Spiral Review and Test Prep 4-2

Circle the correct answer.

1. Which is an INCORRECT writing of the time shown on the clock?

A. two thirty-seven
B. 23 minutes before 2
C. 37 minutes after 2
D. 2:37

2. Evaluate the expression for *n* = 5.

$n \times 7$

A. 2   **C.** 35
B. 12   **D.** 75

3. Multiply.

11×6

A. 5   **C.** 66
B. 17   **D.** 77

4. Complete the table. Write the rule.

In	2	3	5	7	t
Out		12	20		

_____

_____

5. Andy rowed 7 mi on the first day of the week and added 3 mi each day. Make a table and use it to find out how many miles he rowed on the eighth day.

_____

Spiral Review and Test Prep 4-3

Circle the correct answer.

1. Which quadrilateral has 4 sides that are all the same length?

A. Rectangle
B. Trapezoid
C. Square
D. Parallelogram

2. Find the missing number.

$5 \times 7 = $ _____ $\times 5$

A. 4   **C.** 6
B. 5   **D.** 7

3. Which number completes the fact family?

_____ $\times 7 = 42$

$7 \times$ _____ $= 42$

$42 \div$ _____ $= 7$

$42 \div 7 = $ _____

A. 6   **C.** 4
B. 5   **D.** 3

Write and answer the hidden question. Then solve the problem.

4. A puzzle book has 6 puzzles on a page and 8 pages in a chapter. Megan did half the problems in the chapter. How many puzzles did she do?

_____

_____

_____

5. Look for a pattern. Tell the missing numbers.

1, 3, 6, 8, 11, 13, 16,

_____ , _____ , _____

Write >, <, or = for each _____ .

6. 100 hours _____ 4 days

7. 16 weeks _____ 5 months

Spiral Review and Test Prep 4-4

Circle the correct answer.

Write and answer the hidden questions. Then solve the problem.

1. Solve the equation for $z \div 4 = 4$ by testing these values for z: 4, 8, 12, and 16.

A. 4   **C.** 12
B. 8   **D.** 16

4. A small restaurant has 6 tables that each seat 4 people. It also has 5 tables with seating for 6 people. How many people can the restaurant seat altogether?

2. Multiply.

$$\begin{array}{r} 8 \\ \times\ 9 \\ \hline \end{array}$$

A. 62
B. 63
C. 72
D. 73

_____

_____

3. Tara got on a train at 9:30 A.M. She arrived at her destination 1 hr and 47 min later. What time did she arrive?

A. 11:07 A.M.
B. 11:17 A.M.
C. 11:07 P.M.
D. 11:17 P.M.

_____

_____

_____

Write >, <, or = for each ____.

5. 52 weeks ____ 365 days

6. 4 decades ____ 50 years

Spiral Review and Test Prep 4-5

Circle the correct answer.

1. Evaluate the expression for $y = 6$.

   $y + y$

   A. 12   **C.** 1
   B. 6   **D.** 0

2. Multiply.

   $$\begin{array}{r} 11 \\ \times\ 11 \\ \hline \end{array}$$

   A. 101
   B. 110
   C. 111
   D. 121

3. An array has 6 rows of 8 squares. Which of the following arrays does not have the same number of squares?

   A. 1 row of 48 squares
   B. 2 rows of 20 squares
   C. 4 rows of 12 squares
   D. 8 rows of 6 squares

Channel	9:00	9:30	10:00	10:30	11:00	11:30
2			Cooking		Travel	
3		Football				
4	Pets	Baseball				

4. Which show lasts for the shortest period?

   _____

Complete the table below to solve the problem.

5. Two woodworkers each work a 9-hr day. The first spends 2 hr setting up his tools. Then he makes 1 cabinet every hour. The second spends 1 hr setting up her tools and then makes 1 cabinet every other hour. Who made more cabinets by the end of the day?

	1	2	3	4	5	6	7	8	9
Worker 1	0	0	1	2					
Worker 2	0	1							

_____

Name_____

Spiral Review and Test Prep 4-6

Circle the correct answer.

JULY

S	M	T	W	T	F	S
	1	2	3	4	5	6
7	8	9	10	11	12	13
14	15	16	17	18	19	20
21	22	23	24	25	26	27
28	29	30	31			

1. Jill bought 4 boxes of granola bars. There are 8 bars in each box. How many granola bars did she buy?

A. 40 **C.** 24

B. 32 **D.** 16

2. Solve the equation for t. Test these values for t: 1, 2, 3, 4.

$t \times 10 = 30$

A. 1 **C.** 3

B. 2 **D.** 4

3. Which expression cannot be used to solve $57 + 49$?

A. $(57 + 50) - 1$

B. $(57 + 50) + 1$

C. $(57 + 43) + 6$

D. $(51 + 49) + 6$

4. What date is 2 weeks after July 2?

_____

5. What date is 10 days after July 14?

_____

Write and answer the hidden question. Then solve the problem.

6. Leon buys 4 six-packs of juice for $12.00. How much did each container of juice cost him?

_____

_____

Name _____

Spiral Review and Test Prep 4-7

1. John planted 50 plants in 5 equal rows. How many plants are in each row?

   A. 5   **C.** 15

   B. 10   **D.** 20

Mountain	Inches of Snow
Skytop	✳ ✳ ✳ ✳
Eagle	✳ ✳ ✳ ✳ ✳
Carl	✳ ✳ ✳ ✳ ✳
Lanier	✳ ✳ ✳

Each ✳ = 1 in. of snow.

2. Evaluate for $n = 4$.

   $(3n) - 2$

   A. 12   **C.** 10

   B. 11   **D.** 9

5. How many inches of snow does Mt. Carl have?

_____

3. Which is not part of the fact family for 7, 8, and 56?

   A. $7 \times 8 = 56$

   B. $7 + 8 = 56$

   C. $56 \div 7 = 8$

   D. $8 \times 7 = 56$

Write and answer the hidden question. Then solve the problem.

Ticket	Rides per Ticket	Price
A	5	$5.00
B	10	$8.00

6. Tom buys two B tickets. How much did Tom spend?

_____

_____

_____

4. Evaluate for $k = 3$.

   $27 \div k$

   A. 3   **C.** 9

   B. 7   **D.** 24

Name_____

Spiral Review and Test Prep 4-8

Circle the correct answer.

1. Subtract.

   $52.23
   − 12.25
   _____

   A. $37.98
   B. $38.98
   C. $39.98
   D. $40.98

2. Which expression has the same answer as $(6 + 6 + 6 + 6) − 3$?

   A. $(6 \times 6) + 3$
   B. $(4 \times 6) − 3$
   C. $(4 \times 6) + 3$
   D. $(4 \times 4) − 3$

3. Solve the equation for t. Test these values for t: 5, 6, 7, 8.

   $2t + 1 = 15$

   A. 5   C. 7
   B. 6   D. 8

4. Multiply.

   12×5

   A. 40   C. 55
   B. 50   D. 60

Lisa counted the peas in 17 peapods and recorded the data in a line plot.

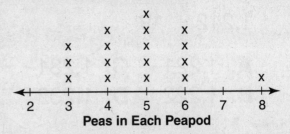

Peas in Each Peapod

5. What is the most common number of peas in a peapod?

   _____

Complete the table below to solve the problem.

6. Two chefs are preparing lunch. The first cracks 2 eggs every 5 seconds. The second chef cracks 3 eggs every 10 seconds. How long will it take them to crack 21 eggs?

Seconds	10		
Cook 1	4	8	
Cook 2	3		

Spiral Review and Test Prep 4-9

Circle the correct answer.

1. Add. Use mental math.

$1{,}212 + 19$

A. 1,221   **C.** 1,231
B. 1,222   **D.** 1,232

2. David has 3 boards. He wants to have 6 boards of equal length. Each board is 16 ft long. How long should he cut each board?

A. 2 ft   **C.** 6 ft
B. 4 ft   **D.** 8 ft

3. Evaluate the expression for $d = 0$.

$(7 \times d) + 7$

A. 0   **C.** 7
B. 1   **D.** 14

4. Divide.

$99 \div 9$

A. 11
B. 10
C. 9
D. 8

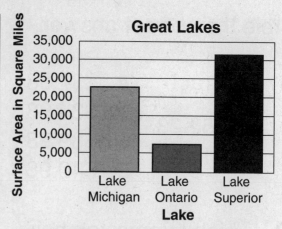

Great Lakes

5. Which lake has the greatest surface area?

_____

Write and answer the hidden question. Then solve the problem.

6. Alice bought 3 yellow roses. How much did she spend?

Rose	Price
Yellow	$3.00
Red	$4.00

_____

_____

_____

_____

Spiral Review and Test Prep 4-10

Circle the correct answer.

1. Find the elapsed time.

   Start: 1:43 A.M.
   Finish: 6:20 A.M.

   A. 4 hr 17 min
   B. 4 hr 27 min
   C. 4 hr 37 min
   D. 4 hr 47 min

2. Evaluate the expression for $z = 5$.

   $3z + 3$

   A. 21   C. 15
   B. 18   D. 12

3. Which is 43,466 rounded to the hundreds place?

   A. 43,400   C. 43,500
   B. 43,470   D. 44,000

4. Multiply.   A. 63
                   B. 65
   7×9 C. 69
                   D. 72

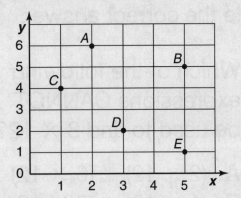

Name the ordered pair for each point.

5. B _____

6. C _____

7. E _____

Write and answer the hidden question. Then solve.

8. An ice machine makes 8 pieces of ice in a half hour. How many pieces of ice does it make in 2 hours?

   _____

   _____

   _____

Spiral Review and Test Prep 4-11

Circle the correct answer.

1. Which of the following expressions CANNOT be used to find 8×12?

  A. $(2 \times 12) + (6 \times 12)$
  B. $(1 \times 12) + (8 \times 12)$
  C. $(6 \times 12) + (2 \times 12)$
  D. $(3 \times 12) + (5 \times 12)$

2. Use breaking apart to find 9×8.

  A. 64   **C.** 81
  B. 72   **D.** 90

3. Solve the equation for k. Test these values for k: 9, 10, 11, 12.

  $9 \times k = 99$

  A. 9   **C.** 11
  B. 10   **D.** 12

4. Multiply.

    $\begin{array}{r} 12 \\ \times\ 7 \\ \hline \end{array}$

  A. 60
  B. 77
  C. 72
  D. 84

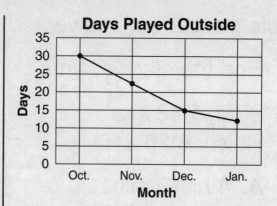

Days Played Outside

Daniel recorded how many days each month he played outside. He then plotted the data on a line graph.

5. In which month did he play the least number of days outside?

_____

Complete the table to solve the problem.

6. Mario draws three pictures each day. How many pictures would he draw in 5 days?

Days	1	2	3	4	5
Pictures	3				

_____

Spiral Review and Test Prep 4-12

Circle the correct answer.

1. How many months are in a century?

   A. 10×100
   B. 12×100
   C. $10 \times 1{,}000$
   D. $12 \times 1{,}000$

2. Evaluate the expression for $t = 3$.

   $8t - 2$

   A. 12   C. 18
   B. 16   D. 22

3. Which is not part of the fact family for 3, 10, and 30?

   A. $3 \times 10 = 30$
   B. $30 \div 10 = 3$
   C. $10 \times 3 = 30$
   D. $30 \times 10 = 3$

Day	Number of Diners
Monday	10
Tuesday	20
Wednesday	35
Thursday	50

4. Complete the line graph using the data from the table.

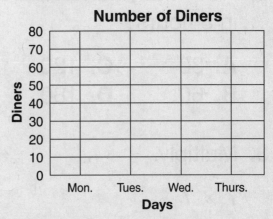

Write and answer the hidden question. Then solve.

5. Airline A needs seats for 3 of their planes. Each plane needs 12 rows of seats with 2 seats in each row. How many new seats does Airline A need to buy?

_____

_____

Spiral Review and Test Prep 4-13

Circle the correct answer.

1. Which is a correct expression for $(z + z + z)$?

    A. 3   **C.** $3z$

    B. z **D.** $3 \div z$

2. How many minutes are in 3 hours?

    A. 30   **C.** 120

    B. 60   **D.** 180

3. Multiply.

    7×7

    A. 47   **C.** 70

    B. 49   **D.** 77

4. Subtract.

       $246.11
    $-$ 50.12

    A. $199.99

    B. $195.99

    C. $195.98

    D. $195.89

Write and answer the hidden question. Then solve the problem.

5. Nell tries 4 different flavors of juice each week at the local juice shop. The shop has 28 different flavors. How many weeks will it take for her to try all flavors?

_____

_____

6. Find the median, mode, and range of the set of data.

    22, 22, 25, 35, 40, 22, 23, 42, 26, 27, 30

_____

_____

7. Evaluate the expression for $k = 11$.

    $5 \times k$

_____

Spiral Review and Test Prep 4-14

Circle the correct answer.

1. Charles left home at 3:45 P.M. He arrived home 1 hr and 38 min later. What time did he arrive home?

   A. 5:13 A.M.
   B. 5:13 P.M.
   C. 5:23 P.M.
   D. 6:23 A.M.

2. Which shows $7 + 7 + 7 + 7 + 7 + 7 = 42$ as a multiplication sentence?

   A. $7 \times 7 = 49$
   B. $6 \times 7 = 42$
   C. $5 \times 7 = 35$
   D. $4 \times 6 = 24$

3. Which shows the Commutative Property of Multiplication?

   A. $3 \times 0 = 0$
   B. $4 \times 3 = 12$
   C. $1 \times 9 = 9$
   D. $9 \times 3 = 3 \times 9$

Write and answer the hidden question. Then solve the problem.

4. A bag of charcoal has 180 pieces of charcoal. Ken uses 60 pieces each time he grills. How many times can Ken grill with 1 bag of charcoal?

   _____

   _____

   _____

Favorite Sport to Play

Football	ⅢⅢ I
Baseball	ⅢⅢ ⅢⅢ ⅢⅢ I
Basketball	ⅢⅢ ⅢⅢ ⅢⅢ ⅢⅢ
Hockey	ⅢⅢ I
Soccer	ⅢⅢ ⅢⅢ ⅢⅢ ⅢⅢ ⅢⅢ

5. According to the data, which type of sport is the favorite to play?

   _____

Spiral Review and Test Prep 4-15

Circle the correct answer.

1. Add.

$$\begin{array}{r} 5,481 \\ 2,018 \\ 34 \\ +\quad 189 \\ \hline \end{array}$$

A. 8,722
B. 7,750
C. 7,722
D. 6,782

2. Solve the equation by testing these values for x: 2, 4, 6, and 8.

$2x \div 4 = 3$

A. 2   C. 6
B. 4   D. 8

3. Evaluate the expression for $z = 12$.

$10z$

A. 140   C. 110
B. 120   D. 100

Complete the table to solve the problem.

4. Jay jogged for 15 min on Day 1. He plans to jog 10 min longer each day than the previous day. For how many min will he jog on day 5?

Day	1	2	3	4	5
Min	15	25			

_____

5. Why is the graph misleading?

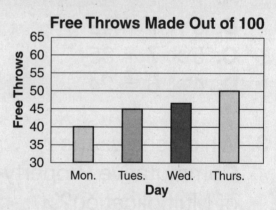

_____

_____

_____

Spiral Review and Test Prep 5-1

Circle the correct answer.

1. How many seconds are in two minutes?

    A. 30   **C.** 120

    B. 60   **D.** 180

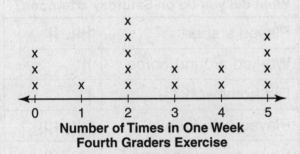

Number of Times in One Week
Fourth Graders Exercise

2. How many times do most fourth graders exercise during the week?

    A. 2   **C.** 4

    B. 3   **D.** 5

3. What is the mode for this set of data?

12, 18, 16, 17, 16, 15, 14

    A. 6   **C.** 15

    B. 12   **D.** 16

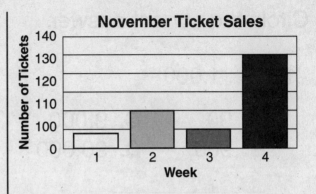

November Ticket Sales

4. Looking at the graph, about how many times as many tickets does it seem were sold in week 2 as in week 3?

_____

5. Why is the graph misleading?

_____

6.

How many lines of symmetry does this figure have?

_____

Name_____

Spiral Review and Test Prep 5-2

Circle the correct answer.

1. 9 × 1,000

   A. 90   **C.** 9,000

   B. 900   **D.** 90,000

June						
S	M	T	W	T	F	S
						1
2	3	4	5	6	7	8
9	10	11	12	13	14	15
16	17	18	19	20	21	22
23	24	25	26	27	28	29
30						

2. Which date is two weeks after June 6th?

   A. June 19th

   B. June 20th

   C. June 21st

   D. June 22nd

3. Which date is one week before June 25th?

   A. June 5th

   B. June 11th

   C. June 18th

   D. June 30th

4. Fill in the blanks. To find 6 × 6,000, multiply _____ and _____. Then write _____ zeros at the end.

What did you do on Saturday afternoon?	
Played a sport	卌 II
Worked around home	II
Did homework	I
Played with friends	卌 卌 I
Spent time with family	卌 III

5. How many more students played with friends than did homework?

_____

6.

Write if the angle is right, acute, or obtuse.

_____

Name _____

Spiral Review and Test Prep 5-3

Circle the correct answer.

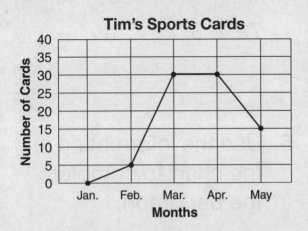

Tim's Sports Cards

1. During which month did Tim have exactly 15 sports cards?

A. February **C.** April
B. March **D.** May

2. How many cards did Tim add to his collection between March and April?

A. 25 **C.** 5
B. 15 **D.** 0

3. Subtract.

$\frac{6}{7} - \frac{2}{7}$

A. $\frac{4}{7}$ **C.** $\frac{4}{0}$
B. $\frac{8}{7}$ **D.** $\frac{8}{14}$

4. 5×31 is close to

$5 \times$ _____.

5. 8×683 is close to

$8 \times$ _____.

Train Number	1501	1502	1503	1504
DEPART Chicago	7:00 A.M.	9:35 A.M.	1:15 P.M.	4:45 P.M.
ARRIVE Detroit	11:00 A.M.	1:50 P.M.	5:45 P.M.	9:00 P.M.

6. Write two statements comparing the times in the train schedule.

_____

_____

_____

_____

_____

Compare. Write >, <, or = for each _____.

7. 56,724 _____ 56,742

8. 3,892,201 _____ 3,892,102

Name_____

Spiral Review and Test Prep 5-4

Circle the correct answer.

1. Which of the following means the same as 8:36?

    A. Quarter to eight
    B. Thirty-five minutes past eight
    C. Twenty-four minutes after eight
    D. Twenty-four minutes to nine

2. Evaluate the expression for $n = 6$.

    $8n$

    A. 14   **C.** 28
    B. 24   **D.** 48

Use mental math to find the product.

3. 4×56

    A. 224   **C.** 196
    B. 204   **D.** 164

4. Multiply.

    79×3

_____

5. Use the information in the chart to complete the bar graph.

Fourth Graders' Favorite Sport

Sport	Number of Votes
Football	25
Basketball	20
Soccer	30

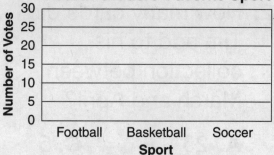

6. How many more students voted for soccer than football?

_____

Name_____

Spiral Review and Test Prep 5-5

Circle the correct answer.

1. Yolanda set up an array of beans on the table. The array had 16 rows. Each row had 4 beans. How many beans were there in all?

A. 12   **C.** 48
B. 20   **D.** 64

2. Find the range for this set of data.

34, 34, 32, 31, 27, 39, 37

A. 12   **C.** 34
B. 31   **D.** 39

3.

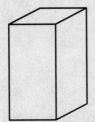

How many faces does the figure have?

A. 4   **C.** 8
B. 6   **D.** 12

A factory makes three different products.

Number Produced in	Product A	Product B	Product C
1 hr	18	18	20
2 hr	40	42	28
3 hr	52	60	34

4. How long does it take to make 52 of Product A?

_____

5. Write two statements comparing how long it takes to make the products.

_____

_____

_____

_____

_____

_____

Spiral Review and Test Prep 5-6

Circle the correct answer.
Find each product.

Day	Number Repaired
Monday	8
Tuesday	5
Wednesday	7
Thursday	4
Friday	3

1.   64
      × 5

A. 69
B. 309
C. 315
D. 320

2.   88
      × 7

A. 616
B. 606
C. 416
D. 406

5. Pete made a table to show how many bikes Kerry repaired at his bike repair shop. On which two days did Kerry repair the most bikes?

_____

_____

3.

What time is shown on the clock?

A. 9:14   **C.** 3:44
B. 8:15   **D.** 3:15

6.

Estimate the amount that is shaded.

_____

4. How many weeks are there in 3 years?

_____

Spiral Review and Test Prep 5-7

Circle the correct answer.

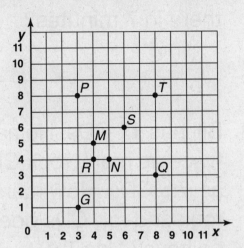

4. Use the data in the chart to complete the pictograph.

Chess Club Victories January–March

Player	Victories
Sven	4
Nikolai	12
Evan	0
Tenille	7
Sarah	8

1. What is the ordered pair for point *M?*

A. (4, 5)   **C.** (5, 4)

B. (3, 4)   **D.** (4, 4)

2. What point is located at (3, 8)?

A. *P*   **C.** *S*

B. *Q*   **D.** *T*

Chess Club Victories, January–March

Sven	
Nikolai	
Evan	
Tenille	
Sarah	

Each ☐ = 2 victories.

3. Multiply.

$$523 \times 6$$

A. 1,578
B. 1,589
C. 3,138
D. 3,149

5.
$$706 \times 7$$

6. Write a fraction equivalent to $\frac{3}{5}$.

Name_____

Spiral Review and Test Prep 5-8

Circle the correct answer.

Track Meet A	Track Meet B
8:00 Start	10:00 Start
8:30 Mile run	10:15 High jump
9:00 100 yd dash	11:00 Mile run
1:00 Hurdles	1:00 Hurdles

1. Karen compared the schedules of two track meets. Which statement is true?

   A. Both meets start at 10:00.
   B. Both have the mile run as the first event.
   C. Both have hurdles at 1:00.
   D. Both have the 100 yd dash at 9:00.

2. What is the median of this set of data?

   2, 2, 1, 10, 8, 14, 9

   A. 2   C. 13
   B. 8   D. 14

3. How many seconds are there in 7 minutes?

   _____

4. Bill has 12 CDs. He has twice as many rock CDs as rap CDs. How many rock and rap CDs does he have? Use Try, Check, and Revise to solve.

   _____

5. Find the product.

   $$\begin{array}{r} 472 \\ \times\ \ \ 9 \\ \hline \end{array}$$

6. Draw a figure congruent to Figure A.

   Figure A

Spiral Review and Test Prep 5-9

Circle the correct answer.

1. Which is a longer length of time than 4 hours?

   A. 160 min **C.** 220 min
   B. 185 min **D.** 245 min

2. Which ordered pair would be highest on the graph?

   A. (1, 2)   **C.** (6, 2)
   B. (1, 6)   **D.** (2, 8)

3. Divide.

   $3\overline{)46}$

   A. 13 R2
   B. 14 R3
   C. 15 R1
   D. 16

4. A number cube has the numbers 10, 12, 13, 14, 15, and 16. What is the probability of tossing an even number?

   A. 4 out of 6
   B. 2 out of 6
   C. 1 out of 4
   D. 0 out of 6

5. Use the data to complete the line graph.

Tina's Bowling Scores

Month	Score
September	40
October	45
November	35
December	40

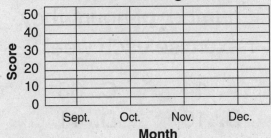

Tina's Bowling Scores

Find each product. Tell what computation method you used.

6.   5,864
      $\times$ 6
     _____

7.   2,003
      $\times$ 3
     _____

Spiral Review and Test Prep 5-10

Circle the correct answer.

Hours of Exercise Each Week

Hours	Votes
4	~~THH~~ ~~THH~~ II
5	~~THH~~ II
6	~~THH~~ ~~THH~~ IIII

1. How many people were surveyed about the number of hours they exercise each week?

A. 14　　C. 33

B. 16　　D. 41

2. How many people exercised 6 hours per week?

A. 14　　C. 33

B. 16　　D. 41

3. Which number makes the statement true?

$16 - \underline{\quad} < 12$

A. 2　　C. 4

B. 3　　D. 5

Find each product.

4.　　$\begin{array}{r} \$4.67 \\ \times \quad 8 \\ \hline \end{array}$

5.　　$\begin{array}{r} \$23.55 \\ \times \quad 6 \\ \hline \end{array}$

Stop	Park	A	B	C	D	Library
Bus 7	8:00	—	8:15	8:30	—	9:00
Bus 9	8:00	—	—	8:15	8:25	8:40

6. Write two statements comparing the times in the bus schedule.

_____

_____

_____

_____

_____

_____

Name_____

Spiral Review and Test Prep 5-11

Circle the correct answer.

Multiply.

1. 4 × 8 × 25

    A. 800   **C.** 425

    B. 640   **D.** 300

2. 3 × 400 × 5

    A. 600   **C.** 6,000

    B. 3,200   **D.** 7,200

3. The machine ran from 7:05 A.M. to 6:35 P.M. For how long did the machine run?

    A. 30 min

    B. 1 hr, 30 min

    C. 11 hr, 30 min

    D. 12 hr, 25 min

4. How would you write $4\frac{2}{10}$ as a decimal?

    A. 0.42   **C.** 4.02

    B. 4.042   **D.** 4.2

5. Use the chart to complete the bar graph.

Age of U.S. Presidents When Inaugurated

President	Age
John Tyler	51
Ronald Reagan	69
Theodore Roosevelt	42

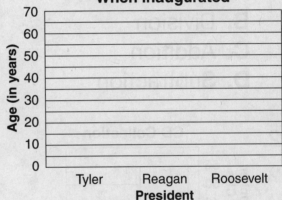

Age of U.S. Presidents When Inaugurated

6. Who was the youngest when inaugurated?

_____

7. $6.34 = _____ dollars +

_____ dimes +

_____ pennies

6.34 = _____ ones +

_____ tenths +

_____ hundredths

Spiral Review and Test Prep 5-12

Circle the correct answer.

If there are 60 min in 1 hr, how many minutes are there in 4 hours?

1. What operation would you use to solve this problem?

   A. Multiplication
   B. Division
   C. Addition
   D. Subtraction

2.

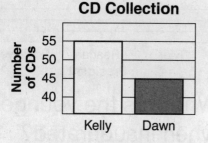

CD Collection

Why is this graph misleading?

   A. There are two different bars.
   B. The vertical scale does not begin at 0.
   C. Both bars extend past 40.
   D. It is labeled incorrectly.

Draw a picture to show the main idea. Then solve the problem.

3. Dario saved 15 quarters and 7 times as many dimes. How many dimes did he save?

_____

House Painting Schedule	
8:30–10:30	Patch cracks
10:30–12:00	Paint gutters
12:00–12:30	Lunch
12:30–5:30	Paint walls

4. Will the painters spend more time patching cracks or painting walls?

_____

Spiral Review and Test Prep 6-1

Circle the correct answer.

Find each product. Use mental math.

1. 8 × 1,000

   A. 80   **C.** 8,000

   B. 800   **D.** 80,000

2. 12 × 100

   A. 1,200

   B. 12,000

   C. 120,000

   D. 1,200,000

Estimate each product.

3. 96 × 4

   A. 400   **C.** 250

   B. 300   **D.** 200

4. 28 × 3

   A. 30   **C.** 90

   B. 33   **D.** 110

Use Try, Check, and Revise to solve the problem.

5. Carl has a hat collection. He has twice as many fishing hats as baseball hats. He has 9 hats total in his collection. How many of each hat does he have?

_____

_____

6. Find the median, mode, and range of this set of data.

62   60   50   53   54
55   50   57   64

_____

7. Order the decimals from greatest to least.

0.07   0.12   0.09   0.5

_____

Spiral Review and Test Prep 6-2

Circle the correct answer.

1. 8 × 2 × 50

    A. 800   **C.** 550

    B. 600   **D.** 400

2. Which fraction is equivalent to $\frac{2}{3}$?

    A. $\frac{3}{4}$ **C.** $\frac{4}{8}$

    B. $\frac{6}{9}$ **D.** $\frac{6}{12}$

3. $\begin{array}{r} \$2.44 \\ \times\ \ \ \ 8 \\ \hline \end{array}$

    A. $13.52

    B. $16.52

    C. $19.52

    D. $22.52

4. How would you write $\frac{12}{100}$ as a decimal?

    A. 1.12   **C.** 0.12

    B. 1.2   **D.** 0.012

Draw a picture to show the main idea. Then choose an operation and solve the problem.

5. Roland was born in 1986. How old was he in 2003?

_____

Multiply. Use mental math.

6. 50 × 20

_____

7. 30 × 600

_____

Spiral Review and Test Prep 6-3

Circle the correct answer.

Find each product. Decide if your answer is reasonable.

1.   17
   $\times$ 8

     A. 136
     B. 135
     C. 129
     D. 95

2.   53
   $\times$ 5

     A. 58
     B. 265
     C. 270
     D. 275

3. Which statement best describes the chances that a plant will grow all the way to the moon?

     A. Certain
     B. Likely
     C. Unlikely
     D. Impossible

Use Try, Check, and Revise to solve the problem.

4. Together, Mario and Gina have $20. Gina has three times as much money as Mario. How much money does each person have?

_____

_____

Estimate each product by finding a range.

5. 58×12

_____

_____

6. 239×48

_____

_____

Spiral Review and Test Prep 6-4

Circle the correct answer.

Find each product. Estimate to check for reasonableness.

1. $\begin{array}{r} 523 \\ \times \quad 7 \end{array}$

   A. 3,661
   B. 3,611
   C. 1,361
   D. 530

2. $\begin{array}{r} 707 \\ \times \quad 9 \end{array}$

   A. 5,454
   B. 5,473
   C. 6,363
   D. 6,373

3. Add.

   $\frac{1}{5} + \frac{3}{5}$

   A. $\frac{4}{10}$ C. $\frac{2}{5}$

   B. $\frac{4}{5}$ D. $\frac{1}{4}$

4. How many grams are in 7 kilograms?

   A. 7   C. 700
   B. 70   D. 7,000

5. What four simpler problems can you use to find 32×45?

   _____

   _____

   _____

   _____

   Draw a picture to show the main idea. Then choose an operation and solve the problem.

6. If there are 60 sec in 1 min, how many seconds are there in 7 minutes?

   _____

Spiral Review and Test Prep 6-5

Circle the correct answer.

Multiply.

1. $5 \times 6 \times 5$

    A. 16   **C.** 35
    B. 30   **D.** 150

2. $200 \times 4 \times 4$

    A. 3,200   **C.** 1,600
    B. 2,400   **D.** 1,200

Divide.

3. $18 \div 2$

    A. 6   **C.** 12
    B. 9   **D.** 36

4. $16 \div 4$

    A. 8   **C.** 4
    B. 6   **D.** 2

Make an organized list to solve the problem.

5. Jim needs to go to the store, the library, and the bakery. He can go to these places in any order he wants. How many different orders are possible?

_____

_____

_____

Use Try, Check, and Revise to solve the problem.

6. In Mrs. Henderson's class, there are two times as many girls as boys. There are 21 students in the class. How many boys and girls are there?

_____

_____

Spiral Review and Test Prep 6-6

Circle the correct answer.

1. Estimate how full the cylinder is.

A. About full
B. About one-fourth full
C. About half full
D. About three-fourths full

Multiply.

2. 45
× 29

A. 1,305
B. 1,265
C. 1,205
D. 1,065

3. 78
× 13

A. 1,114
B. 1,014
C. 1,004
D. 944

Use Try, Check, and Revise to solve the problem. Write the answer.

Fishing Equipment

Hooks	$0.25
Line	$1.00
Sinkers	$0.50

4. Fred spent $2.25. He bought 5 of one item and 1 other item. What did he buy?

_____

_____

Find each product. Use mental math.

5. 6 × 900

_____

6. 5,000 × 7

_____

Spiral Review and Test Prep 6-7

Circle the correct answer.

1. A bag has 5 white marbles and 3 green marbles. What is the probability of picking a green marble?

   A. 3 out of 5
   B. 8 out of 8
   C. 3 out of 8
   D. 5 out of 8

2. Estimate the product.

   716 × 32

   A. 210   C. 21,000
   B. 2,100   D. 24,000

3. Multiply.   A. 9,028
                  B. 8,628
       148   C. 8,028
     × 61   D. 8,026

4. Find the product.

   93 × 5

   A. 155   C. 468
   B. 465   D. 555

Draw a picture to show the main idea. Then choose an operation and solve the problem.

5. In 1961, the record for the most home runs in one season was 61. In 2001, the record was 73 home runs. By how much did the record increase?

_____

6. Kelly read 488 pages in March. The entire fourth grade read 37 times that many pages. How many total pages did the entire fourth grade read in March?

_____

Name_____

Spiral Review and Test Prep 6-8

Circle the correct answer.

1. Multiply.

$$
\begin{array}{r}
187 \\
\times\ 56 \\
\hline
\end{array}
$$

A. 10,472
B. 9,482
C. 9,480
D. 8,470

2. Evaluate the expression for $n = 8$.

$n \div 8$

A. 1   **C.** 16
B. 8   **D.** 64

Use mental math to find each product.

3. 39×5

A. 85
B. 145
C. 195
D. 250

4. 8×62

A. 412
B. 456
C. 496
D. 502

Use Try, Check, and Revise to solve the problem.

Hiking Trails

Trail	Number of Miles
A	5
B	7
C	12
D	20

5. Dario hiked one of the trails twice, then hiked another trail one time. He hiked a total of 29 miles. Which two trails did he hike? Which trail did he hike twice?

_____

_____

Multiply. Tell what computation method you used.

6.
$$
\begin{array}{r}
300 \\
\times\ 30 \\
\hline
\end{array}
$$

_____

Spiral Review and Test Prep 6-9

Circle the correct answer.

1. What is the value of the underlined digit?

4<u>6</u>7,729

A. 6   C. 6,000
B. 600   D. 60,000

2. A hexagon has six sides. Each side is 4 in. long. What is the hexagon's perimeter?

A. 26 in.   C. 14 in.
B. 24 in.   D. 10 in.

3. Multiply.

$$\begin{array}{r} \$3.64 \\ \times\ \ \ 27 \\ \hline \end{array}$$

A. $82.26
B. $88.28
C. $96.28
D. $98.28

4. What is the product of 233 and 5?

A. 1,165   C. 1,345
B. 1,255   D. 2,065

Draw a picture to show the main idea. Then choose an operation and solve the problem.

5. Donna sold books for $0.10 each. How much money did she have if she sold 8 books?

_____

6. There are 24 students in the class. Each paid $2.20 to go on the field trip. How much money did the teacher collect?

_____

7. Into what two simpler problems can you break apart 6 × 24?

_____

Spiral Review and Test Prep 6-10

Circle the correct answer.

1. Estimate the product.

6 × 391

A. 2,400 **C.** 2,600
B. 2,500 **D.** 2,700

2. Divide.

6)48

A. 4
B. 8
C. 12
D. 16

3. Multiply.

58
× 5

A. 290
B. 263
C. 260
D. 63

4. Multiply.

$6.87
× 17

A. $105.59
B. $106.69
C. $115.89
D. $116.79

Solve the problem. Show your computation.

5. A touchdown is worth 6 points. Davis scored two touchdowns in his first game and three touchdowns in his second game. How many total points did he score?

_____

_____

_____

_____

Use Try, Check, and Revise to solve the problem.

6. Louise is twice as old as her younger brother John. Their combined ages are 45. How old is each person?

_____

_____

Spiral Review and Test Prep 7-1

Circle the correct answer.

1. Wayne bought 6 football tickets. Each ticket cost $26. How much money did he spend?

A. $144   **C.** $152
B. $150   **D.** $156

2. An average-sized manatee can eat about 150 lb of food per day. How much food can a manatee eat in 30 days?

A. 4,500   **C.** 6,500
B. 5,000   **D.** 9,000

3. Multiply.

$306 \times 42 =$

A. 12,872   **C.** 12,452
B. 12,852   **D.** 12,382

4. Multiply.

$48 \times 51 =$

A. 2,448   **C.** 2,584
B. 2,548   **D.** 2,844

Solve the problem. Show your computation.

5. Mugs cost $2.35 each. How much would it cost to buy 6 mugs?

_____

_____

6. Richard ran 2 km. How many meters did Richard run?

_____

7. Round 6,852 to the nearest thousand.

_____

Spiral Review and Test Prep 7-2

Circle the correct answer.

1. Find the quotient.

$48,000 \div 6 =$

A. 8   C. 800

B. 80   D. 8,000

2. A science museum hosted a school field trip. There were 23 classes and 19 students in each class. How many students visited the museum?

A. 437   C. 439

B. 438   D. 443

3. Estimate the product.

47×8

A. 200   C. 350

B. 300   D. 400

4. Round 45,682 to the nearest thousand.

A. 45,680   C. 46,000

B. 45,700   D. 50,000

Solve the problem. Show your computation.

5. Peter pounded 129 nails on Monday and 171 on Tuesday. Chris pounded 132 on Wednesday and 169 on Thursday. Which person pounded more nails?

6. In basketball, a basket made from outside of the arc scores 3 points. Bill made 7 of these shots in his first game and 4 in his second game. How many total points did he score?

Name_____

Spiral Review and Test Prep 7-3

Circle the correct answer.

1. Estimate.

$299 \div 6$

A. 49   **C.** 51

B. 50   **D.** 54

2. Multiply.

$\begin{array}{r} 123 \\ \times \ 74 \end{array}$

A. 8,712
B. 8,892
C. 9,002
D. 9,102

3. Divide. Use mental math.

$420 \div 6 =$

A. 7   **C.** 700

B. 70   **D.** 7,000

4. Evaluate $(n + 3) \times 2$ for $n = 4$.

A. 12   **C.** 16

B. 14   **D.** 19

Solve the problem. Show your computation.

5. Kerry went out to dinner. She ordered shrimp for $14.59, salad for $5.77, and 2 lemonades for $1.25 each. How much money did she spend altogether?

6. Estimate the product.

69×898

_____

7. Solve the equation $7k - 1 = 20$ by testing for these values: 0, 1, 2, 3.

_____

Spiral Review and Test Prep 7-4

Circle the correct answer.

1. Each box holds 30 glasses. There are 94 glasses and 3 boxes. How many extra glasses are there?

   A. 4   **C.** 2

   B. 3   **D.** 1

2.

Which point is at (9, 7)?

   A. *A*   **C.** *D*

   B. *G*   **D.** *F*

3. Multiply.

   341 × 18

   A. 6,158   **C.** 6,138

   B. 6,148   **D.** 6,128

Make an organized list to solve the problem.

4. Joe does push-ups, sit-ups, and jumping jacks. He does these in a different order every day. How many different orders are possible?

_____

5. Estimate the quotient.

   555 ÷ 68

_____

6. Multiply.

$$\begin{array}{r} \$5.37 \\ \times32 \\ \hline \end{array}$$

_____

Spiral Review and Test Prep 7-5

Name_____

Circle the correct answer.

1. Divide.

9)187

 A. 21 R7
 B. 20 R7
 C. 19 R8
 D. 19 R7

2.

What time is shown on the clock?

 A. 2:12 **C.** 3:12
 B. 2:15 **D.** 3:22

3. Multiply.

20 × 4,100 =

 A. 8,200 **C.** 82,000
 B. 8,300 **D.** 92,000

Solve the problem. Show your computation.

4. The fourth graders are going on a field trip. Mr. Smith's class has 6 groups of 4 students. Mr. Weller's class has 5 groups of 5 students. How many students total are going on the field trip?

5. Divide.

4)33

6. Multiply.

$$\begin{array}{r} 78 \\ \times\ \ 45 \\ \hline \end{array}$$

Spiral Review and Test Prep 7-6

Circle the correct answer.

1. Marcus puts an equal number of baseball cards into 6 boxes. He has 86 cards. How many cards are in each box and how many are left over?

A. 14 R2   **C.** 14 R5
B. 14 R4   **D.** 14 R6

2. Divide.

$4\overline{)89}$

A. 21 R1
B. 21 R2
C. 22 R1
D. 22 R3

3. If 15 schools of fish each had 16 fish in them, how many fish are there altogether?

A. 225   **C.** 240
B. 230 R3   **D.** 245 R1

Make an organized list to solve the problem.

4. Doreen can wear her fleece or jean jacket as a coat. For a hat, she can wear her baseball hat, knit cap, or dress hat. How many different coat-hat combinations can she make?

_____

5. Estimate the product.

27×39

_____

6. Add.

$$\begin{array}{r} 6.92 \\ + \ 3.45 \\ \hline \end{array}$$

Name_____

Spiral Review and Test Prep 7-7

Circle the correct answer.

1. Multiply.

562
× 62

A. 34,821
B. 34,844
C. 34,894
D. 35,824

2. Seven students are planning to take an exercise class. If the cost is $12 per student, how much will all the students pay for one class?

A. $86   **C.** $82
B. $84   **D.** $80

3. Divide.

4)79

A. 19
B. 19 R1
C. 19 R2
D. 19 R3

Solve the problem. Show your computation.

4. Kelly needs to buy 2 front-row tickets for $35.50 each and 2 bleacher tickets for $15.25 each. How much money will she spend on tickets?

5. Scott has $49 and would like to buy some models. Each model costs $9. How many models can he buy? How much more money will he need to buy another model?

_____

_____

Name_____

Spiral Review and Test Prep 7-8

Circle the correct answer.

1. Divide.

$6\overline{)381}$
   A. 63 R3
   B. 63 R4
   C. 64
   D. 64 R3

2. Multiply.

634
× 25
   A. 15,440
   B. 15,460
   C. 15,750
   D. 15,850

3. How would you write $4\frac{5}{10}$ as a decimal?

   A. 4.5   **C.** 0.45
   B. 4.05   **D.** 0.045

4. Estimate the product.

208 × 12

   A. 1,500   **C.** 2,000
   B. 1,700   **D.** 2,500

Solve the problem. Show your computation.

5. Each bat bag can hold about 10 to 12 baseball bats. If the team has 3 full bat bags, about how many bats are there to choose from?

6. A tandem is a bicycle that two people ride at the same time. If 49 people want to ride tandems, how many tandems would be needed? How many people would not be able to ride?

_____

_____

_____

Spiral Review and Test Prep 7-9

Circle the correct answer.

1. Joe is 56th in line. Marty is 2 places behind him. What place in line is Marty?

A. 54th   **C.** 58th
B. 57th   **D.** 59th

2. Divide.

$2\overline{)412}$

A. 210
B. 209
C. 206
D. 204

3. Divide.

$7\overline{)841}$

A. 120 R1
B. 119 R2
C. 119
D. 118

4. Multiply 60×30.

A. 1,200   **C.** 1,800
B. 1,500   **D.** 2,400

Make an organized list to solve the problem.

5. Gary is going to use two different colors to paint his room. His choices are blue, olive, tan, gray, and purple. How many different combinations can he make?

_____

6. Multiply. Then tell whether you used mental math, paper and pencil, or a calculator.

$$\begin{array}{r} 2{,}561 \\ \times 44 \\ \hline \end{array}$$

_____

Spiral Review and Test Prep 7-10

Circle the correct answer.

1. An 8-pack of yogurt is on sale for $2.80. How much does each yogurt cost?

    A. $0.45   **C.** $0.35
    B. $0.40   **D.** $0.30

2. Multiply. Use mental math.

$50 \times 7,000 =$

    A. 350,000 **C.** 35,000
    B. 320,000 **D.** 3,500

3. What is the standard form for four thousand, two hundred ninety-six?

    A. 4,096   **C.** 4,296
    B. 4,196   **D.** 4,920

4. Divide.

    $7\overline{)1,421}$ **A.** 203
                  B. 204
                  C. 205 R3
                  D. 206 R4

Make an organized list to solve the problem.

5. How many different ways can three friends, Allen, Matthew, and Roger, sit in the backseat of a car?

_____

6. Lane has 16 times as much money as Sven. Sven has $3.57. How much money does Lane have?

_____

7. Find the elapsed time. Start time: 8:45 A.M. End time: 2:15 P.M.

_____

Spiral Review and Test Prep 7-11

Circle the correct answer.

1. Which of the following is the correct number sentence for the problem below?

Francis bought 3 lb of red delicious apples for $2.97. How much was each pound of apples?

- **A.** $3.97 ÷ 3 = n$
- **B.** $2.97 ÷ 3 = n$
- **C.** $2.97 ÷ 2 = n$
- **D.** $297 ÷ 3 = n$

2. Divide.

$9\overline{)\$3.60}$

- **A.** $0.30
- **B.** $0.40
- **C.** $0.45
- **D.** $0.49

3. Estimate the product.

91×27

- **A.** 2,800
- **C.** 2,600
- **B.** 2,700
- **D.** 2,500

Solve the problem. Show your computation.

4. Emily kicks a soccer ball every day. On Saturday she did 12 kicks with her left foot and 18 with her right foot. On Sunday she did 22 with her left foot and 25 with her right foot. How many total kicks did she do?

5. Multiply.

$$\begin{array}{r} 163 \\ \times\ \ 89 \\ \hline \end{array}$$

6.

Are the figures congruent?

Spiral Review and Test Prep 7-12

Circle the correct answer.

1. Which list of numbers is divisible by 2?

    A. 6, 8, 9, 10
    B. 6, 8, 10, 14
    C. 6, 8, 11, 14
    D. 5, 8, 10, 14

2. Multiply mentally.

    $80 \times 700 =$

    A. 4,900   **C.** 49,000
    B. 5,600   **D.** 56,000

3.

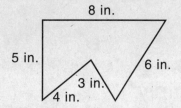

Find the perimeter.

    A. 22 in.   **C.** 26 in.
    B. 24 in.   **D.** 28 in.

4. $15 \times 36 =$

    A. 51   **C.** 540
    B. 380   **D.** 612

Solve the problem. Show your computation.

5. Blaine and Craig shot basketballs. Blaine shot 87 baskets in the first hour and Craig shot 96. In the second hour, Blaine shot 78 baskets and Craig shot 68. Did they shoot more baskets the first hour or the second hour?

6. Write a number sentence. Ali went to a bookstore. He bought 4 books for $24.52. How much did each book cost?

_____

_____

Spiral Review and Test Prep 7-13

Circle the correct answer.

1. A student's test scores are 87, 89, 80, 93, and 76. Find the average.

   A. 75   **C.** 86

   B. 85   **D.** 95

2. Multiply.

$$\begin{array}{r} 361 \\ \times\ 74 \\ \hline \end{array}$$

   A. 25,724

   B. 26,604

   C. 26,624

   D. 26,714

3.

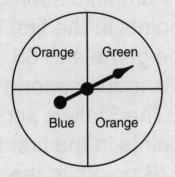

What is the probability the spinner will land on blue?

   A. $\frac{1}{4}$ **C.** $\frac{3}{4}$

   B. $\frac{2}{4}$ **D.** $\frac{4}{4}$

Make an organized list to solve the problem.

4. A team has four different jerseys and four different pants. The patterns of each are stripes, checks, dark, and light. How many different combinations can the team wear?

_____

5. Is 334 divisible by 3? How can you tell?

_____

_____

6. Estimate the product.

57 × 57

_____

Spiral Review and Test Prep 7-14

Circle the correct answer.

1. There are about 500 times as many species of ants as there are termites. There are about 40 species of termites. How many species of ants are there?

 A. 2,000
 B. 20,000
 C. 200,000
 D. 2,000,000

2. Divide. Use mental math.

 $350 \div 50 =$

 A. 4   C. 6
 B. 5   D. 7

3. Multiply 39×65.

 A. 2,520   C. 2,530
 B. 2,525   D. 2,535

4. Kelsey practiced piano for 7 days. On Monday, she practiced for 5 min. Each day she added 5 more minutes. What was the average number of minutes she practiced?

_____

Solve the problem. Show your computation.

5. The Ramblers scored 45 points in the first half of the game and 65 points in the second half. The Staleys scored 36 points in the first half and 76 points in the second half. Which team won the game?

Name_____

Spiral Review and Test Prep 7-15

Circle the correct answer.

1. Divide.

$36\overline{)842}$

    A. 23 R14
    B. 23 R12
    C. 22 R14
    D. 21 R14

2. What is $\frac{1}{8}$ of 40?

    A. 5   **C.** 12
    B. 10   **D.** 18

3. Multiply.

$$\begin{array}{r} \$2.75 \\ \times\ \ \ \ \ 3 \\ \hline \end{array}$$

    A. $8.55
    B. $8.45
    C. $8.35
    D. $8.25

4. Divide.

$80\overline{)5,680}$

    A. 7 R80
    B. 70
    C. 71
    D. 71 R8

Solve the problem. Show your computation.

5. Jim needs 27 boxes. The boxes cost $2.89 each. He also needs box tape, which costs $3.59. How much money will he have to spend?

6. Multiply. Then tell the computation method you used.

$800 \times 30 =$

_____

Name_____

Spiral Review and Test Prep 8-1

Circle the correct answer.

1. Which list of numbers is divisible by three?

 A. 6, 9, 18, 25
 B. 6, 9, 21, 24
 C. 6, 9, 20, 24
 D. 6, 9, 14, 24

2. Three friends went out for breakfast. The total bill was $18.51. They each paid the same amount. Which expression shows how much each person paid?

 A. $18.51 ÷ 4
 B. $18.51 ÷ 3
 C. $18.51 ÷ 2
 D. $18.52 ÷ 3

3. Which of the following expressions shows *Nine girls less than a number of boys went to camp*?

 A. *n* − 9 **C.** *n* − 12
 B. *n* − 3 **D.** 9 − *n*

4. Is 513 divisible by 9?

_____

5.

April						
S	M	T	W	T	F	S
	1	2	3	4	5	6
7	8	9	10	11	12	13
14	15	16	17	18	19	20
21	22	23	24	25	26	27
28	29	30				

What date is one week before April 26?

_____

Estimate each quotient. Tell whether you found an overestimate or underestimate.

6. 187 ÷ 4

_____

_____

7. 609 ÷ 7

_____

_____

Spiral Review and Test Prep 8-2

Circle the correct answer.

1. Find the average. A student's test scores are 78, 89, 93, and 76.

    A. 84   **C.** 86
    B. 85   **D.** 87

2. Which pair of numbers is divisible by 9?

    A. 342, 135
    B. 123, 456
    C. 555, 888
    D. 111, 202

3. What shape are the faces of a cube?

    A. Circle   **C.** Square
    B. Triangle **D.** Pyramid

4. Which is the best estimate for the product of 58 × 89?

    A. 5,400   **C.** 5,200
    B. 5,300   **D.** 5,100

5. Divide.

$$11\overline{)246}$$

A group of backpackers is carrying a total of 26 packets of trail mix. There are 4 backpackers on the trip.

6. If the packets are divided up equally, how many packets will each backpacker carry?

_____

7. How many extra trail mix packets will there be?

_____

8. What is the average of the set of data?

121, 134, 125, 156

_____

Spiral Review and Test Prep 8-3

Circle the correct answer.

1. How many more sides does an octagon have than a hexagon?

A. 4   **C.** 2
B. 3   **D.** 1

2. Will is taking his twin teenage sons skiing for their birthday. Each ski lift pass costs $32.25. If all 3 of them go skiing, how much will it cost?

A. $96.00   **C.** $96.50
B. $96.25   **D.** $96.75

3. How many edges does a rectangular pyramid have?

A. 4   **C.** 7
B. 5   **D.** 8

Write a number sentence to solve the problem.

4. There are 88 students in fourth grade. There are 4 different fourth-grade classes. How many students are in each class?

_____

_____

_____

_____

5. $7\overline{)94}$

Divide. Use mental math.

6. $5,600 \div 80 =$

_____

Name_____

Spiral Review and Test Prep 8-4

Circle the correct answer.

1. A honeybee can fly about 15 mi per hour. How far can the honeybee fly in 3 hr if it flies continuously?

    A. 12 mi   **C.** 36 mi
    B. 18 mi   **D.** 45 mi

2. How many vertices does a pentagon have?

    A. 4   **C.** 6
    B. 5   **D.** 8

3. 30, 15, 45, and 50 are all divisible by what number?

    A. 2   **C.** 5
    B. 3   **D.** 4

4. Divide.

    $9\overline{)47}$

    A. 5
    B. 5 R2
    C. 6
    D. 6 R2

5. Each CD rack can hold 8 CDs. Karen has 66 CDs. How many CD racks does Karen need? How many CDs will be on the rack that is not filled?

_____

_____

6. Draw a pair of lines that are intersecting but not perpendicular.

7. Aaron wants to buy four computer games. Each game costs $39.00. How much money will he spend?

_____

Name_____

Spiral Review and Test Prep 8-5

Circle the correct answer.

1. Which of the following is NOT a parallelogram?

   A. Square
   B. Trapezoid
   C. Rhombus
   D. Rectangle

2.

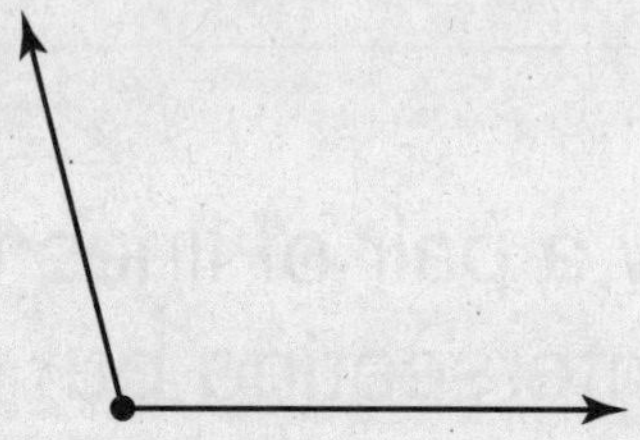

Which geometric term describes what is shown above?

   A. Obtuse angle
   B. Intersecting lines
   C. Acute angle
   D. Ray

3. Divide.

   $6\overline{)1,229}$

   A. 204 R4
   B. 204 R5
   C. 204 R6
   D. 205 R3

Write a number sentence to solve the problem.

4. A pack of cards costs $2.15. If Vera buys 8 packs, how much will she spend?

_____

_____

_____

5. Divide.

   $6\overline{)39}$

6. How many children picked strawberries as their favorite fruit?

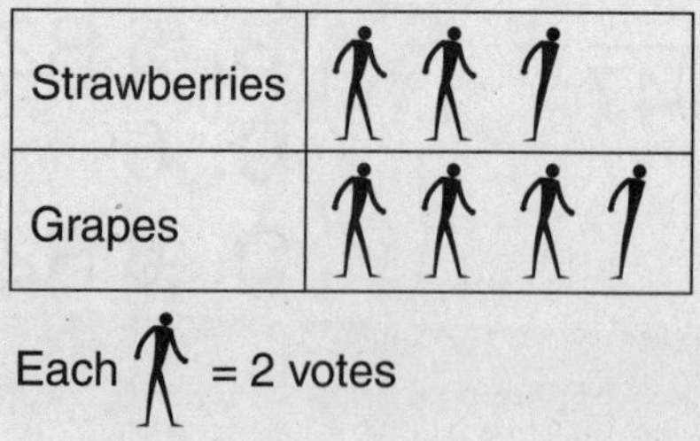

| Strawberries | 🧍 🧍 🧍 |
| Grapes | 🧍 🧍 🧍 🧍 |

Each 🧍 = 2 votes

100   Use with Lesson 8-5.

Name_____

Spiral Review and Test Prep 8-6

Circle the correct answer.

1. If the radius of a circle is 15 cm, how long is its diameter?

   A. 20 cm   C. 35 cm
   B. 30 cm   D. 45 cm

2. Which of the following is an overestimate for $429 \div 6$?

   A. 75   C. 65
   B. 70   D. 60

3. Evaluate $n + 67$ when $n = 25$.

   A. 92   C. 52
   B. 62   D. 542

4. Round 821,965 to the nearest hundred thousand.

   A. 700,000
   B. 800,000
   C. 850,000
   D. 900,000

5. Draw a scalene right triangle.

Write a number sentence to solve the problem.

6. Bats cost $23.50. Mitts cost $35.00. How much will it cost to buy 2 mitts and 1 bat?

   _____

   _____

   _____

7. Three boys plan to contribute an equal amount of money in order to buy a present. The present costs $48.75. How much will each boy contribute?

   _____

Name_____

Spiral Review and Test Prep 8-7

Circle the correct answer.

1.

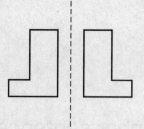

How are the figures related?

A. Slide   **C.** Turn

B. Flip   **D.** Rotation

2. Hannah has five $1 bills, 3 quarters, and 4 dimes. How much money does she have?

A. $6.45   **C.** $6.25

B. $6.35   **D.** $6.15

3. Divide.

$14\overline{)295}$

A. 21

B. 21 R1

C. 22 R1

D. 22 R2

Write a number sentence to solve the problem. Write the answer in a complete sentence.

4. Dinesh has 4 close friends. He gives each friend 13 stickers as a gift. How many stickers does Dinesh give away?

_____

_____

_____

5.

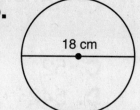

18 cm

What is the radius of the circle?

_____

6. Divide. Use mental math.

$72,000 \div 900 =$

_____

Spiral Review and Test Prep 8-8

Circle the correct answer.

1.

How many lines of symmetry does the figure have?

A. 4   **C.** 2
B. 3   **D.** 1

2. Divide.

5)93

A. 183
B. 88
C. 18 R3
D. 18

3. Divide.

3)459

A. 151
B. 153
C. 156
D. 157

4.

Do the figures appear to be congruent? If so, tell if they are related by a flip, slide, or turn.

_____

5. The camper has 6 storage compartments. Each compartment can hold 3 sleeping bags. If there are 17 sleeping bags to be stored, how many compartments will be used? How many sleeping bags will be in the compartment that is not filled?

_____

_____

_____

_____

_____

Spiral Review and Test Prep 8-9

Circle the correct answer.

1. Alana started her dance lesson at 6:15 P.M. She finished at 7:35 P.M. How long was her lesson?

   A. 1 hr 30 min
   B. 1 hr 20 min
   C. 1 hr 10 min
   D. 1 hr 5 min

2. Divide. Use mental math.

   $360 \div 60 =$

   A. 600   C. 6
   B. 60   D. 1

3.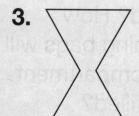

   How many lines of symmetry does the figure have?

   A. 0   C. 2
   B. 1   D. 3

4.

   Do the figures appear to be similar? If so, are they also congruent?

   _____

5. Test 360 to see if it is divisible by 2, 3, 5, 9, or 10.

   _____

Write a number sentence to solve the problem.

6. There are 45 seats in the theater. There are 5 rows. How many seats are in each row?

   _____

   _____

   _____

Spiral Review and Test Prep 8-10

Circle the correct answer.

1. Divide.

$9\overline{)747}$

   A. 84 R2
   B. 84
   C. 83 R2
   D. 83

2. If the ages of three people are 15, 21, and 12, what is the average age?

   A. 18   **C.** 16
   B. 17   **D.** 13

3. Paul makes toy boats. Each boat uses 3 strips of balsa wood. If Paul has 22 strips, how many boats can he make? How many extra strips will he have after making the boats?

   A. 7 boats, 1 strip
   B. 6 boats, 4 strips
   C. 7 boats, 4 strips
   D. 8 boats, 0 strips

Group 1   Group 2

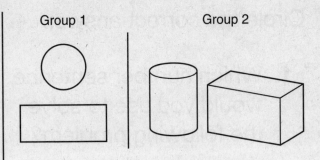

4. Write two statements describing how the figures in Group 1 and Group 2 are alike.

_____

_____

_____

5. Draw two rectangles that are similar but not congruent.

Spiral Review and Test Prep 8-11

Circle the correct answer.

1. Which number sentence would you use to solve the following problem?

   Jerry has 150 lb of concrete that he must move. If each wheelbarrow load can handle 25 lb, how many loads must he take?

   A. $150 + 25 = n$
   B. $n - 25 = 150$
   C. $n \times 5 = 25$
   D. $150 \div 25 = n$

2. Divide.

   $6\overline{)55}$

   A. 9
   B. 9 R1
   C. 9 R2
   D. 9 R3

3. Divide. Use mental math.

   $320 \div 40 =$

   A. 360   C. 80
   B. 280   D. 8

4. Compare an equilateral triangle to an isosceles triangle.

   _____

   _____

   _____

   _____

   _____

   _____

   _____

   _____

   _____

   _____

5.

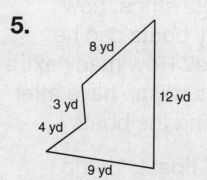

   What is the perimeter of the figure?

   _____

Name_____

Spiral Review and Test Prep 8-12

Circle the correct answer.

1. Which number sentence would you use to solve the following problem?

A $10 roll of quarters holds 40 quarters. How many quarters are there in three $10 rolls?

A. $40 \times 3 = n$
B. $40 \div 3 = n$
C. $\$10 + \$10 = n$
D. $3 \times \$10 = n$

2. What is the perimeter of a hexagon if each side is 16 ft long?

A. 72 ft   **C.** 106 ft
B. 96 ft   **D.** 116 ft

3. Divide.

$35\overline{)630}$

A. 20
B. 19
C. 18
D. 17

4.

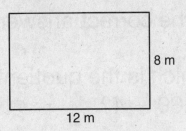

8 m

12 m

What is the area of the rectangle?

_____

5. Mario has 68 picture frames. He hangs an equal number of pictures on the 4 walls of his study. How many pictures are on each wall?

_____

6. Round 6,852 to the nearest thousand.

_____

Name_____

Spiral Review and Test Prep 8-13

Circle the correct answer.

1. Which is the quotient of $4.80 ÷ 4?

   A. $1.20   **C.** $1.40
   B. $1.30   **D.** $1.50

2. Divide.

   $56\overline{)284}$

   A. 4 R12
   B. 5
   C. 5 R4
   D. 5 R16

3. A picture is 8 in. wide and 10 in. high. What is the area of the picture?

   A. 18 sq in.
   B. 28 sq in.
   C. 36 sq in.
   D. 80 sq in.

4. What is the decimal for twenty-five hundredths?

   A. 2,500   **C.** 0.25
   B. 1.25   **D.** 0.025

Write a number sentence to solve the problem.

5. A pharmacist is filling a prescription for a man who needs to take medicine for 10 days. He needs to take 3 tablets per day. How many tablets should the pharmacist give the man?

_____

_____

6. Four friends, Laurel, Sophia, Bridgette, and Charlotte, want to hold hands forming a circle. If Laurel is next to Charlotte, how many different ways can they form a circle?

_____

_____

Spiral Review and Test Prep 8-14

Circle the correct answer.

1.

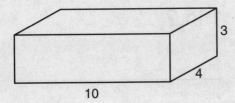

What is the volume of the figure?

A. 17 cubic units

B. 43 cubic units

C. 120 cubic units

D. 240 cubic units

2. Add.

$\frac{1}{8} + \frac{6}{8} =$

A. $\frac{7}{16}$ C. $\frac{5}{8}$

B. $\frac{7}{8}$ D. $\frac{1}{4}$

3. Divide.   A. 11

$7\overline{)78}$ B. 11 R1

     C. 12

     D. 12 R1

4. The tour train car has 6 seats in each row. The train car holds 348 people. How many rows are there?

_____

Write a number sentence to solve the problem.

5. Bill is 3 times older than Dan. If Dan is 7, how old is Bill?

_____

_____

6. Marcus earned a total of $150 doing odd jobs. He worked a total of 5 days. How much did he earn per day?

_____

Spiral Review and Test Prep 9-1

Circle the correct answer.

1. Which is the shape of the flat surface of a cup?

   A. Square
   B. Rectangle
   C. Circle
   D. Pentagon

2. Which list of numbers is divisible by nine?

   A. 6, 9, 18, 27
   B. 9, 18, 27, 36
   C. 6, 9, 20, 24
   D. 6, 9, 14, 24

3. Which solid figure does a soup can look like?

   A. Pyramid
   B. Cube
   C. Cone
   D. Cylinder

4. What is the volume of a cube if each side is 1 in.?

   _____

5. In one section of a baseball stadium, there are 15 rows. There are a total of 90 seats in the section. How many seats are in each row?

   _____

   _____

6. Use geometric terms to describe how cubes and squares are alike.

   _____

   _____

   _____

   _____

Name_____

Spiral Review and Test Prep 9-2

Circle the correct answer.

1. Which fraction of the circle is shaded?

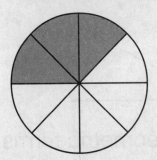

A. $\frac{3}{8}$ **C.** $\frac{5}{8}$

B. $\frac{4}{8}$ **D.** $\frac{6}{8}$

2. Estimate the product of 59 × 189.

A. 14,000 **C.** 11,000
B. 12,000 **D.** 10,000

3. How much taller is the Washington Monument than Napoleon's Column in Paris?

Napoleon's Column in Paris	150 ft
Washington Monument	600 ft

A. 350 ft **C.** 450 ft
B. 400 ft **D.** 500 ft

4. How many faces of a triangular prism are rectangles?

_____

5.

What is the volume of this figure?

_____

6. Find the area of a rectangle with a length of 3 in. and a width of 2 in.

_____

7. Describe how a cylinder and a cone are alike.

_____

_____

_____

Spiral Review and Test Prep 9-3

Circle the correct answer.

1. If a city is divided into halves by a river, with one side flat and the other side hilly, which part of the city is hilly?

   A. $\frac{0}{2}$ C. $\frac{2}{2}$

   B. $\frac{1}{2}$ D. $1\frac{1}{2}$

2. Out of a set of 9 girls, 3 have brown eyes, 2 have green eyes, and 4 have blue eyes. Which fraction of the girls have blue eyes?

   A. $\frac{2}{9}$ C. $\frac{4}{9}$

   B. $\frac{3}{9}$ D. $\frac{5}{9}$

3. Six boys' heights are 48 in., 50 in., 52 in., 45 in., 57 in., and 54 in. What is the average height of the boys?

   A. 51 in.   C. 55 in.
   B. 52 in.   D. 58 in.

4. How many sides does an octagon have?

   _____

5.

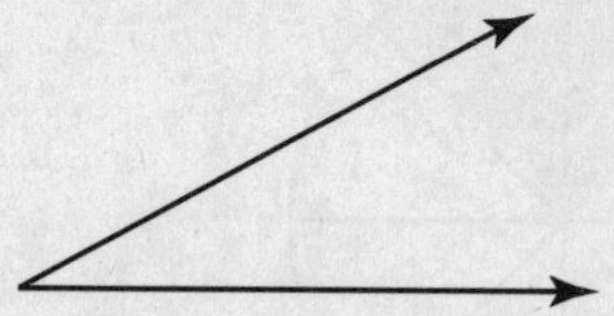

   Use geometric terms to describe what is shown above. Be as specific as possible.

   _____

6. Liz has 6 quarters, 5 dimes, and 10 pennies. Jake has 4 more quarters, no dimes, and 2 fewer pennies. How much money does Jake have?

   _____

Spiral Review and Test Prep 9-4

Circle the correct answer.

1. Which fraction is between $\frac{1}{5}$ and $\frac{3}{5}$ on a number line?

   A. $\frac{1}{10}$ **C.** $\frac{4}{5}$

   B. $\frac{2}{5}$ **D.** $\frac{7}{10}$

2. What passes through the center of a circle?

   A. Diameter

   B. Radius

   C. Axis

   D. Solid

3. A grocer sold 3 of his 10 watermelons. What fraction of his watermelons did he sell?

   A. $\frac{2}{10}$ **C.** $\frac{4}{10}$

   B. $\frac{3}{10}$ **D.** $\frac{5}{10}$

4. Name two polygons that have four vertices and four sides.

_____

_____

5. Describe how the solids in each group are different.

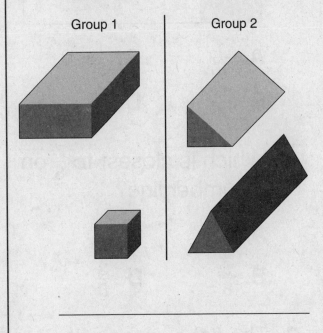

Group 1   Group 2

_____

_____

_____

_____

_____

_____

Spiral Review and Test Prep 9-5

Circle the correct answer.

1. Which is the best estimate for the shaded part?

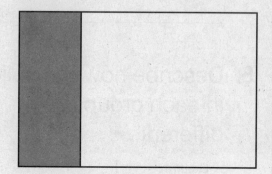

A. $\frac{1}{10}$ **C.** $\frac{1}{5}$

B. $\frac{1}{6}$ **D.** $\frac{1}{4}$

2. Which is closest to $\frac{7}{8}$ on a number line?

A. 1   **C.** $\frac{4}{8}$

B. $\frac{5}{8}$ **D.** $\frac{3}{8}$

3. The flat surface of a cone is shaped like which plane figure?

A. Pentagon
B. Triangle
C. Hexagon
D. Circle

4.

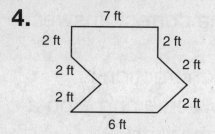

Find the perimeter.

_____

5. Use geometric terms to describe how Figure A and Figure B are different.

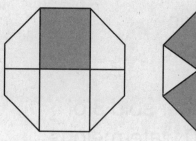

Figure A   Figure B

_____

_____

_____

_____

_____

Spiral Review and Test Prep 9-6

Circle the correct answer.

1. Laura ran a mile in 7 min 34 sec. Stephanie ran a mile in 7 min and 15 sec. How much faster was Stephanie than Laura?

   A. 19 sec **C.** 12 sec
   B. 17 sec **D.** 10 sec

2. Which list of numbers is divisible by both 3 and 9?

   A. 3, 6, 9
   B. 15, 18, 27
   C. 3, 30, 90
   D. 9, 18, 27

3. How many lines of symmetry does a rectangle have?

   A. 1   **C.** 3
   B. 2   **D.** 4

4. If a 10 km race has a marker at the start and finish lines as well as at every 2 km, how many markers are there?

   _____

5. Describe a triangle with sides of 9 in., 4 in., and 6 in.

   _____

   _____

6. Estimate the fractional part that is shaded.

   _____

7. If Tyler takes 3 steps for every 2 steps his father takes, how many steps will Tyler take if his father takes 18 steps?

   _____

Spiral Review and Test Prep 9-7

Circle the correct answer.

1. Which fraction is equivalent to $\frac{2}{3}$?

A. $\frac{4}{6}$ C. $\frac{3}{5}$

B. $\frac{2}{5}$ D. $\frac{1}{3}$

2. Multiply.

$467 \times 4 =$

A. 1,869   C. 1,688

B. 1,868   D. 1,668

3. Each pair of socks costs $4.50. If you buy 5 pairs, how much will they cost?

A. $22.00   C. $23.00

B. $22.50   D. $24.50

4. How many lines of symmetry does the numeral 5 have?

A. 0   C. 2

B. 1   D. 5

5. If Simon used 3 cubes in his first tower, 4 in his second, and 5 in his third, how many cubes would you expect him to use to make his 10th tower?

_____

6.

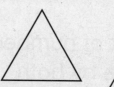 

Do the figures look similar? If so, are they also congruent?

_____

7. Bill is making a clock. He puts a mark at every $\frac{1}{4}$ of the circle. How many marks are there?

_____

Spiral Review and Test Prep 9-8

Circle the correct answer.

1. Which is the area of a square with 8 in. sides?

   A. 72 sq in. **C.** 56 sq in.
   B. 64 sq in. **D.** 32 sq in.

2. Which is the perimeter of a rectangle with sides of 8 ft and 5 ft?

   A. 26 ft   **C.** 16 ft
   B. 24 ft   **D.** 13 ft

3. How many seconds are in 3 min?

   A. 180   **C.** 60
   B. 90   **D.** 30

4. Which number is divisible by both 3 and 5?

   A. 60   **C.** 18
   B. 48   **D.** 12

Write each fraction in simplest form.

5. $\frac{3}{6}$ _____

6. $\frac{5}{15}$ _____

7. Write an equivalent fraction for $\frac{3}{5}$.

_____

8. Use geometric terms to describe how a triangular prism and a pyramid are alike.

_____

_____

_____

_____

_____

Spiral Review and Test Prep 9-9

Circle the correct answer.

1. What are figures that have exactly the same size and shape called?

    A. Similar
    B. Congruent
    C. Different
    D. Related

2. Which fraction in simplest form is $\frac{1}{4}$?

    A. $\frac{3}{12}$ **C.** $\frac{5}{12}$

    B. $\frac{4}{12}$ **D.** $\frac{7}{12}$

3. Which is the area of the rectangle?

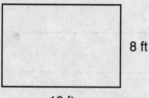

8 ft

12 ft

    A. 48 sq ft
    B. 72 sq ft
    C. 96 sq ft
    D. 108 sq ft

Write > or < for each ◯.

4. $\frac{4}{7}$ ◯ $\frac{5}{7}$

5. $\frac{2}{5}$ ◯ $\frac{2}{10}$

6. Write a number expression for *29 less 5*.

_____

7. Solve the problem. Write your answer in a complete sentence.

Flora bought 11 buttons to sew on her jacket. She wants to put 2 buttons on each of her pockets. If Flora's jacket has 4 pockets, how many buttons will she have left?

_____

_____

_____

_____

Spiral Review and Test Prep 9-10

Circle the correct answer.

1. Which is the volume of a cube with a side of 4 ft?

    A. 64 cubic ft
    B. 60 cubic ft
    C. 16 cubic ft
    D. 12 cubic ft

2. How many lines of symmetry does this figure have?

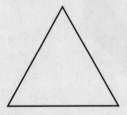

    A. 1   **C.** 3
    B. 2   **D.** 4

3. Which is the decimal for twenty-five hundredths?

    A. 0.25
    B. 0.025
    C. 0.0205
    D. 0.0025

Compare. Write $<$, $>$, or $=$ for each $\bigcirc$.

4. $\dfrac{3}{7}$ $\bigcirc$ $\dfrac{4}{7}$

5. $\dfrac{7}{14}$ $\bigcirc$ $\dfrac{1}{2}$

6. $\dfrac{5}{6}$ $\bigcirc$ $\dfrac{2}{3}$

7. If a hen lays 5 eggs a week, how many eggs does she lay in a year?

_____

8. Use geometric terms to describe how a circle and a sphere are different.

_____

_____

_____

_____

_____

Spiral Review and Test Prep 9-11

Circle the correct answer.

1. Which is the improper fraction for $2\frac{3}{4}$?

    A. $\frac{18}{4}$ **C.** $\frac{11}{4}$

    B. $\frac{12}{4}$ **D.** $\frac{2}{4}$

2. Estimate the product of 33×49.

    A. 1,500   **C.** 1,700
    B. 1,600   **D.** 1,800

3. Divide.

    $723 \div 18 =$

    A. 40 R2   **C.** 40 R8
    B. 40 R3   **D.** 40 R16

4. Which is the product of $8 \times (2 \times 5)$?

    A. 100   **C.** 80
    B. 90   **D.** 70

5. Order the fractions from least to greatest.

    $\frac{5}{8}, \frac{2}{5}, \frac{1}{2}$

_____

6. What is the perimeter of an octagon if each side is 8 in.?

_____

7.

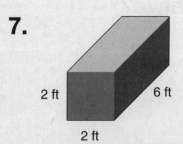

2 ft   6 ft

2 ft

Find the volume.

_____

8. Ben can ride his bike around the block 3 times for each time Hailey can. If Ben rides around the block 12 times, how many times did Hailey ride around the block?

_____

Name_____

Spiral Review and Test Prep 9-12

Circle the correct answer.

1. Which is shown in the figure?

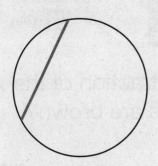

   A. Chord
   B. Radius
   C. Center
   D. Diameter

2. How many acute angles does an equilateral triangle have?

   A. 1   **C.** 3
   B. 2   **D.** 9

3. Which is the mixed number for $\frac{16}{3}$?

   A. $5\frac{1}{3}$ **C.** $5\frac{1}{5}$
   B. $5\frac{2}{5}$ **D.** $3\frac{3}{5}$

Compare. Write <, >, or = for each $\bigcirc$.

4. $1\frac{2}{7}$ $\bigcirc$ $1\frac{2}{3}$

5. $2\frac{1}{4}$ $\bigcirc$ $2\frac{1}{5}$

6. Round 476,852 to the nearest ten thousand.

_____

7. Describe how the two figures are alike using geometric terms.

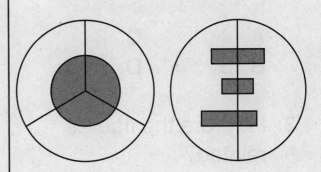

_____

_____

_____

_____

Name_____

Spiral Review and Test Prep 9-13

Circle the correct answer.

1. Which is greater than $3\frac{1}{6}$?

   A. $3\frac{1}{5}$ **C.** $3\frac{2}{12}$

   B. $3\frac{1}{10}$ **D.** $3\frac{1}{12}$

2. How many edges does a square pyramid have?

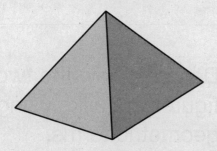

   A. 4   **C.** 8

   B. 5   **D.** 9

3. How are the figures related?

   A. Slide   **C.** Turn

   B. Flip   **D.** Point

4.

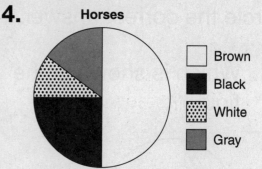

Horses

- Brown
- Black
- White
- Gray

What fraction of the horses are brown?

_____

5. Mary Ann is older than Cynthia. Kyle is younger than Cynthia but older than Darci. Mary Ann is younger than Billy. In what order would the students line up from oldest to youngest?

_____

_____

_____

_____

_____

_____

Name_____

Spiral Review and Test Prep 9-14

Circle the correct answer.

1. Which is the area of a rectangle that is 7 ft wide and 4 ft long?

A. 18 sq ft **C.** 25 sq ft
B. 22 sq ft **D.** 28 sq ft

2. Which of the following has one endpoint?

A. Segment
B. Line
C. Ray
D. Cube

3. What fraction of the circle graph is A?

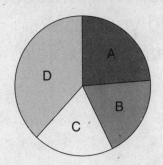

A. $\frac{1}{2}$ **C.** $\frac{1}{4}$

B. $\frac{1}{3}$ **D.** $\frac{1}{8}$

4.

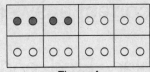

Figure A   Figure B

Explain why both of the pictures show $\frac{1}{4}$ shaded.

_____

_____

_____

_____

_____

_____

5. Use geometric terms to describe how a rectangular prism and a cube are different.

_____

_____

_____

_____

_____

Spiral Review and Test Prep 10-1

Circle the correct answer.

1. Hal, Becky, Fred, and Lindsey lined up for the water fountain. Hal was last in line. Becky was before Lindsey. Fred was not next to Hal. What is the order of the line?

   A. Fred, Hal, Becky, Lindsey

   B. Hal, Fred, Becky, Lindsey

   C. Fred, Lindsey, Hal, Becky

   D. Fred, Becky, Lindsey, Hal

2. Which fraction has blue uniforms?

Soccer Teams' Uniform Colors

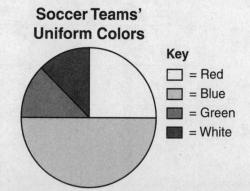

Key
☐ = Red
▨ = Blue
▧ = Green
■ = White

   A. $\frac{1}{2}$ **C.** $\frac{1}{6}$

   B. $\frac{1}{4}$ **D.** $\frac{1}{8}$

3. Order the fractions from greatest to least.

$$\frac{1}{6} \quad \frac{2}{3} \quad \frac{4}{5} \quad \frac{1}{2}$$

_____

4. Write $\frac{4}{20}$ in simplest form.

_____

5. 50 students are asked their favorite sport. 25 say basketball, 13, baseball, and 12, soccer. Draw a circle graph to show the results. What fraction should you label *basketball*? Explain.

_____

_____

_____

Name_____

Spiral Review and Test Prep 10-2

Circle the correct answer.

1. Which sum is LESS than 1?

   A. $\frac{2}{3} + \frac{2}{3}$ C. $\frac{2}{3} + \frac{1}{3}$

   B. $\frac{2}{3} + \frac{1}{6}$ D. $\frac{1}{3} + \frac{4}{3}$

2. What is the mixed number for $\frac{8}{3}$?

   A. $4\frac{2}{3}$ C. $2\frac{2}{3}$

   B. $3\frac{2}{3}$ D. $1\frac{2}{3}$

3. Jonathan's test scores are 88, 79, and 91. What is the average of his scores?

   A. 89   C. 87

   B. 88   D. 86

4. Which is an equivalent fraction to $\frac{3}{7}$?

   A. $\frac{2}{7}$ C. $\frac{6}{14}$

   B. $\frac{5}{14}$ D. $\frac{8}{14}$

5. Each time Ingrid pulls weeds in the garden, her mother gives her $2. If Ingrid's mother gave her $18, how many times did Ingrid pull weeds?

_____

6. Place these fractions in order from least to greatest. Explain how you decided.

   $\frac{1}{12}$ $\frac{1}{4}$ $\frac{1}{10}$ $\frac{1}{2}$ $\frac{1}{3}$ $\frac{1}{6}$

_____

_____

_____

_____

_____

_____

_____

Spiral Review and Test Prep 10-3

Circle the correct answer.

1. In one week a boss paid Mr. Richards $400 and Mr. Carrington $800. What fraction of the total money was paid to Mr. Richards?

   A. $\frac{2}{3}$ C. $\frac{1}{3}$

   B. $\frac{1}{2}$ D. $\frac{1}{4}$

2. Add.

   $\frac{4}{12} + \frac{7}{12} =$

   A. $\frac{11}{12}$ C. $\frac{9}{12}$

   B. $\frac{10}{12}$ D. $\frac{8}{12}$

3. Which is the mode for this data?

   45, 48, 53, 59, 57, 58, 48, 57, 57, 55

   A. 57   C. 46
   B. 48   D. 14

4. Compare. Use $<$, $>$, or $=$.

   $\frac{2}{8} + \frac{1}{8}$ ◯ $\frac{3}{16}$

5. Multiply or divide to find an equivalent fraction.

   $\frac{4}{7}$ _____

6. Estimate what fraction of the circle is shaded. Explain how you made your estimate.

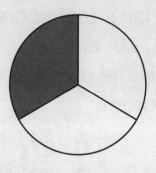

   _____

   _____

   _____

   _____

   _____

Spiral Review and Test Prep 10-4

Circle the correct answer.

1. $\frac{3}{5} + \frac{4}{5} =$

   A. $1\frac{4}{5}$ C. $1\frac{2}{5}$

   B. $1\frac{3}{5}$ D. $1\frac{1}{5}$

2. $\frac{1}{5} + \frac{2}{3} =$

   A. $\frac{14}{15}$ C. $\frac{12}{15}$

   B. $\frac{13}{15}$ D. $\frac{10}{15}$

3. Which is the volume of a rectangular prism with a length of 4 in., a width of 2 in., and a height of 5 in.?

   A. 45 cubic in.
   B. 40 cubic in.
   C. 30 cubic in.
   D. 11 cubic in.

4. Which fraction is $\frac{6}{10}$ closest to on a number line?

   A. $\frac{1}{10}$ C. $\frac{3}{10}$

   B. $\frac{2}{10}$ D. $\frac{1}{2}$

5. Seventy-one hundredths of Earth's surface is covered with water. Write the decimal form for this amount.

   _____

6. A family has 3 daughters and 1 son. What fraction of the children is the son?

   _____

7. Tyler wants to arrange his DVDs on a shelf. The three kinds of DVDs he has are comedy, action, and drama. In how many different ways can Tyler arrange his three kinds of DVDs?

   _____

Spiral Review and Test Prep 10-5

Circle the correct answer.

1. Which is the difference of $\frac{4}{7} - \frac{1}{7}$?

   A. $\frac{1}{7}$ C. $\frac{3}{7}$

   B. $\frac{2}{7}$ D. $\frac{5}{7}$

2. Add.

   $$\frac{1}{2} + \frac{2}{3} =$$

   A. $1\frac{1}{6}$ C. $\frac{4}{6}$

   B. $\frac{5}{6}$ D. $\frac{1}{6}$

3. In a game called four-square, the court is made of a large square divided into 4 smaller squares. If 3 children are playing on 3 of the squares, what part of the large square is missing a player?

   A. $\frac{3}{4}$ C. $\frac{1}{4}$

   B. $\frac{2}{4}$ D. $\frac{0}{4}$

4. At a local animal shelter, there are 21 cats. Seven of them are Siamese cats. What fraction of the cats are Siamese?

   _____

5. Vic is riding his bike from home to the library. He has gone about $1\frac{1}{2}$ mi. Estimate the total distance from Vic's house to the library. Explain how you made your estimate.

Vic is here.

Vic's house   Library

   _____

   _____

   _____

   _____

Spiral Review and Test Prep 10-6

Circle the correct answer.

1. Which is the difference of $\frac{2}{9} - \frac{1}{9}$?

   A. $\frac{1}{9}$ **C.** $\frac{3}{9}$

   B. $\frac{2}{9}$ **D.** $\frac{5}{9}$

2. Subtract.

$$\frac{4}{5} - \frac{2}{3} =$$

   A. $\frac{1}{15}$ **C.** $\frac{3}{15}$

   B. $\frac{2}{15}$ **D.** $\frac{4}{15}$

3. Add.

$$\frac{1}{4} + \frac{3}{8} =$$

   A. $\frac{1}{8}$ **C.** $\frac{4}{8}$

   B. $\frac{2}{8}$ **D.** $\frac{5}{8}$

4. Round 841,333 to the nearest hundred thousand.

   A. 900,000

   B. 800,000

   C. 700,000

   D. 600,000

5. Look for a pattern. Draw the next two figures.

△ □ □ △ □ □ △

6. Write $\frac{12}{5}$ as a mixed number. _____

7. Write $3\frac{2}{3}$ as an improper fraction. _____

Solve. Write the answer in a complete sentence.

8. A grocery shopper bought 4 cartons of eggs. Twelve eggs are in each carton. How many eggs are there in all?

_____

_____

_____

_____

Spiral Review and Test Prep 10-7

Circle the correct answer.

1. There are three rooms, each with a different colored door: red, yellow, and green. A dog, a frog, and a cat are behind the doors. The cat is not behind the red door. The frog is behind the green door. Which door is the dog behind?

   A. Yellow door
   B. Green door
   C. Red door
   D. Blue door

2. Which is the difference of $\frac{2}{3} - \frac{2}{5}$?

   A. $\frac{1}{15}$ C. $\frac{3}{15}$

   B. $\frac{2}{15}$ D. $\frac{4}{15}$

3. Which is the mixed number for $\frac{9}{4}$?

   A. $2\frac{3}{4}$ C. $2\frac{1}{4}$

   B. $2\frac{1}{2}$ D. $1\frac{3}{4}$

4. Dennis cut a peach in half. He then cut each half into 4 equal slices. Dennis ate 4 slices. What fractional part of the peach did Dennis eat?

   _____

   _____

5. Write an equivalent fraction for $\frac{7}{10}$.

   _____

6. Multiply.

   21 × 14 = _____

7. What two plane figures are the faces of a triangular prism?

   _____

   _____

Name_____

Spiral Review and Test Prep 10-8

Circle the correct answer.

1. If the perimeter of a square is 8 ft, what is the length of each side?

A. 1 ft   **C.** 4 ft

B. 2 ft   **D.** 56 ft

2. Which mixed number is equivalent to $\frac{18}{5}$?

A. $1\frac{14}{15}$ **C.** $3\frac{1}{5}$

B. $1\frac{17}{18}$ **D.** $3\frac{3}{5}$

3. How many seconds are in 3 min?

A. 240   **C.** 120

B. 180   **D.** 60

4. Which fraction is equivalent to $\frac{3}{6}$?

A. $\frac{4}{7}$ **C.** $\frac{12}{24}$

B. $\frac{5}{8}$ **D.** $\frac{15}{24}$

5. Karl has four kittens named Earl, Vince, Pete, and Jackson. One is gray, one is brown, one is black, and one is white. Pete is brown. Vince is not white. Jackson is gray. What color is Earl?

_____

6. Place these fractions in order from greatest to least. Explain how you decided.

$$\frac{7}{12} \quad \frac{5}{12} \quad \frac{1}{24} \quad \frac{5}{6} \quad \frac{1}{2}$$

_____

_____

_____

_____

_____

_____

_____

Spiral Review and Test Prep 10-9

Circle the correct answer.

1. Measure a side of the triangle to the nearest $\frac{1}{2}$ inch.

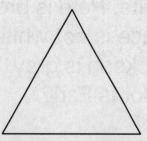

    A. 3 in.   **C.** 2 in.

    B. $2\frac{1}{2}$ in.   **D.** $1\frac{1}{2}$ in.

2. How many miles are in 10,560 ft?

    A. 1 mi   **C.** 3 mi
    B. 2 mi   **D.** 4 mi

3. Which fraction is closest to zero on a number line?

    A. $\frac{1}{2}$ **C.** $\frac{4}{5}$

    B. $\frac{2}{3}$ **D.** $\frac{1}{7}$

4. Compare. Use $<$, $>$, or $=$.

    $\frac{4}{7}$ ◯ $\frac{5}{7}$

5. Write $\frac{3}{18}$ in simplest form.

_____

Solve. Write the answer in a complete sentence.

6. Danielle made a box to store her toys. She needs to buy a cover for the box. The sides are each 3 ft long. What is the area of the cover Danielle needs?

_____

_____

7. Write a number expression for *16 less than 83*.

_____

Spiral Review and Test Prep 10-10

Circle the correct answer.

1. What unit of capacity is equal to $\frac{1}{4}$ gal?

   A. Cup
   B. Half gallon
   C. Quart
   D. Pint

2. All sides of an octagon are $\frac{1}{4}$ in. long. What is the perimeter to the nearest $\frac{1}{2}$ in.?

   A. 1 in.   **C.** 2 in.

   B. $1\frac{1}{2}$ in.   **D.** $2\frac{1}{2}$ in.

3. There are 3 girls wearing red shirts in a class of 24. What fraction of the class are wearing red shirts?

   A. $\frac{1}{7}$ **C.** $\frac{3}{8}$

   B. $\frac{1}{8}$ **D.** $\frac{4}{9}$

4. Compare. Use $<$, $>$, or $=$.

   $1\frac{7}{14}$ ◯ $1\frac{5}{14}$

5. Draw a figure that has at least two lines of symmetry.

6. Estimate the location of the fractions, and draw them on the number line.

   $\frac{1}{5}$ $\frac{6}{7}$ $\frac{1}{3}$ $\frac{3}{4}$

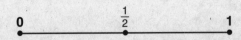

Spiral Review and Test Prep 10-11

Circle the correct answer.

1. How many ounces are in 1 lb?

    A. 15 oz   **C.** 18 oz

    B. 16 oz   **D.** 21 oz

2. Estimate the product of 58×29.

    A. 3,400   **C.** 2,000

    B. 2,600   **D.** 1,800

3. Which is equal to 16 fl oz?

    A. 3 qt   **C.** 1 pt

    B. 2 qt   **D.** 2 pt

4. Subtract.

$$\frac{11}{13} - \frac{5}{13} =$$

    A. $\frac{6}{13}$ **C.** $\frac{8}{13}$

    B. $\frac{7}{13}$ **D.** $\frac{9}{13}$

5. Compare. Use $<$, $>$, or $=$.

$$1\frac{2}{3} \bigcirc 1\frac{4}{6}$$

6. Multiply.

$$11 \times 11 = \underline{\hspace{2cm}}$$

7. Write $3\frac{1}{7}$ as an improper fraction.

_____

Solve. Write the answer in a complete sentence.

8. Hannah, Jake, Lydia, and Cate are in line for the movies. Hannah is between Lydia and Cate. Jake is not last. Who is first in line?

_____

_____

_____

Name_____

Spiral Review and Test Prep 10-12

Circle the correct answer.

1. Which is equal to 8 qt?

   A. 16 pt   **C.** 2 pt
   B. 3 gal   **D.** 16 gal

2. How many pounds are in 32 oz?

   A. 1 lb   **C.** 3 lb
   B. 2 lb   **D.** 4 lb

3. Divide.

$$\$35.70 \div 7 =$$

   A. \$5.20   **C.** \$5.05
   B. \$5.10   **D.** \$5.03

4. Add.

$$432 + 234 + 777 =$$

   A. 1,234   **C.** 1,394
   B. 1,344   **D.** 1,443

5. Ten students out of 90 received a score of 90 or better on a test. Is it reasonable to estimate the fraction of students who received at least a 90 on the test to be about $\frac{1}{10}$? _____

6. Write $\frac{10}{15}$ in simplest form.

_____

7.

Explain why both of the illustrations show $\frac{1}{2}$.

_____

_____

_____

_____

_____

Spiral Review and Test Prep 10-13

Circle the correct answer.

1. How many cups are in 1 gal?

    A. 8 c   **C.** 16 c

    B. 12 c   **D.** 20 c

2. Which is an equivalent fraction for $\frac{1}{4}$?

    A. $\frac{2}{5}$ **C.** $\frac{3}{11}$

    B. $\frac{6}{18}$ **D.** $\frac{9}{36}$

3. Which is the word name for 0.35?

    A. Thirty-five hundredths

    B. Thirty-five

    C. Thirty-five tenths

    D. Thirty-five thousandths

4. Which is the fraction $\frac{10}{24}$ in simplest form?

    A. $\frac{5}{16}$ **C.** $\frac{3}{10}$

    B. $\frac{5}{12}$ **D.** $\frac{3}{8}$

5. Tell whether an exact answer is needed or if an estimate is enough. Then solve.

Mitzi's rope is 25 in. long and Tom's rope is 4 in. long. About what fraction of Mitzi's rope is Tom's rope?

_____

_____

6. A parking lot is putting in new lights. Each row of parking spaces is 100 m long. There are 3 rows. If each row is to have a light pole every 20 m and a light pole at each end, how many light poles are needed for the parking lot?

_____

Name_____

Spiral Review and Test Prep 11-1

Circle the correct answer.

1. Add.

$\frac{1}{8} + \frac{5}{6} =$

A. $\frac{11}{12}$ **C.** $\frac{19}{20}$

B. $\frac{15}{16}$ **D.** $\frac{23}{24}$

2. Which of the following is the sum of $\frac{5}{8} + \frac{7}{8}$?

A. $1\frac{1}{8}$ **C.** $1\frac{1}{2}$

B. $1\frac{1}{4}$ **D.** $1\frac{5}{8}$

3. How many inches are in 1 yd?

A. 12 in. **C.** 36 in.

B. 24 in. **D.** 48 in.

4. Subtract.

$\frac{3}{4} - \frac{1}{3} =$

A. $\frac{5}{12}$ **C.** $\frac{7}{12}$

B. $\frac{1}{2}$ **D.** $\frac{2}{3}$

Write the number in standard form.

5. 200,000 + 50,000 + 600 + 80 + 4

_____

Tell whether an exact answer is needed or if an estimate is enough. Then solve.

6. Tom wants to buy three books. One costs $4.95, another costs $1.50, and the third costs $3.79. If Tom has $15.00, does he have enough money to buy the three books?

_____

Add.

7. 652 + 789 = _____

8. $58 + $98 = _____

Name

Spiral Review and Test Prep 11-2

Circle the correct answer.

1. Add.

$$\frac{2}{6} + \frac{3}{6} =$$

A. $\frac{2}{3}$ **C.** $1\frac{1}{6}$

B. $\frac{5}{6}$ **D.** $1\frac{1}{3}$

2. Which is the sum of $\frac{3}{7} + \frac{6}{7}$?

A. $1\frac{1}{7}$ **C.** $1\frac{3}{7}$

B. $1\frac{2}{7}$ **D.** $1\frac{4}{7}$

3. Multiply.

$$3,042 \times 6 =$$

A. 18,252   **C.** 18,272

B. 18,262   **D.** 18,282

4. Subtract.

$$\frac{9}{11} - \frac{5}{11} =$$

A. $\frac{4}{11}$ **C.** $\frac{7}{11}$

B. $\frac{6}{11}$ **D.** $\frac{8}{11}$

5. Write $\frac{21}{100}$ as a decimal.

_____

6. There are 5 people: Wynn, Vic, Pat, Dan, and Elita. Their ages are 42, 41, 15, 8, and 3. Dan is the oldest and Pat is the youngest. Elita is 15. Wynn is not 8, and he is older than Vic. How old is Vic?

_____

Tell whether an exact answer is needed or if an estimate is enough. Then solve.

7. Jane wants to make 2 recipes. One recipe uses $1\frac{1}{3}$ c flour and the other uses 2 c flour. How much flour does Jane need?

_____

Spiral Review and Test Prep 11-3

Circle the correct answer.

1. Which of the following is the sum of $\frac{2}{5} + \frac{7}{10}$?

    A. $\frac{4}{5}$ C. $1\frac{1}{10}$

    B. $\frac{9}{10}$ D. $1\frac{1}{5}$

2. Add.

    $\frac{3}{8} + \frac{3}{4} =$

    A. $1\frac{1}{8}$ C. $1\frac{3}{8}$

    B. $1\frac{1}{4}$ D. $1\frac{1}{2}$

3. Name the figure.

    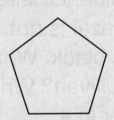

    A. Quadrilateral
    B. Pentagon
    C. Hexagon
    D. Octagon

4. Write 2.25 as a fraction in simplest form.

    _____

5. Write the word form for 6.5<u>9</u> and tell the value of the underlined digit.

    _____

    _____

Tell whether an exact answer is needed or if an estimate is enough. Then solve.

6. Jackie needs 15 lb of gravel to finish landscaping a driveway. She brought loads of $6\frac{1}{2}$ lb, $5\frac{1}{4}$ lb, and $4\frac{3}{4}$ lb. Does Jackie have enough gravel?

    _____

7. Estimate the product of 13×52.

Spiral Review and Test Prep 11-4

Circle the correct answer.

1. Subtract.

$$\frac{5}{6}$$
$$-\frac{1}{6}$$

A. $\frac{2}{3}$ **C.** $\frac{1}{3}$

B. $\frac{1}{2}$ **D.** $\frac{1}{6}$

2. How many ounces are in $\frac{1}{2}$ lb?

A. 3   **C.** 6

B. 4   **D.** 8

3. Multiply.

$26 \times 38 =$

A. 928   **C.** 968

B. 948   **D.** 988

4. Which is the product of 9×4?

A. 39   **C.** 32

B. 36   **D.** 26

5. Write nine and thirty-eight hundredths in standard form.

_____

6. Order the numbers from least to greatest.

4.6, 1.3, 6.2

_____

7. Ryan has 4 fish named Ty, Hazel, Sullivan, and Giselle. One is orange, one black, one white, and one blue. Giselle is orange. Hazel is not blue. Ty is black. What color is Sullivan? Write the answer in a complete sentence.

_____

8. Compare. Use $<$, $>$, or $=$.

$\frac{1}{3}$ ◯ $\frac{2}{3}$

Name_____

Spiral Review and Test Prep 11-5

Circle the correct answer.

1. Divide.

$56 \div 9 =$

A. 6 R1   **C.** 6 R3
B. 6 R2   **D.** 6 R4

2. A chef needs to add
1 fl oz of lemon juice to
a recipe. He does not
have anything that
measures fluid ounces.
What equivalent
measure could he use?

A. 1 tbsp   **C.** 1 tsp
B. 2 tbsp   **D.** 2 tsp

3. Which is the difference
of $\frac{3}{4} - \frac{7}{12}$?

A. $\frac{1}{12}$ **C.** $\frac{1}{4}$
B. $\frac{1}{6}$ **D.** $\frac{1}{3}$

4. Order the numbers from
greatest to least.

3.36, 3.83, 3.63

_____

5. Round 1.37 to the
nearest tenth.

_____

6. Quincy has a 10 ft
board to cut into 12
equal pieces. How long
should each piece be?
Write the answer in a
complete sentence.

_____

Write each fraction in
simplest form.

7. $\frac{9}{12}$ _____

8. $\frac{10}{15}$ _____

9. $\frac{6}{8}$ _____

Spiral Review and Test Prep 11-6

Circle the correct answer.

1. Classify the triangle by its sides.

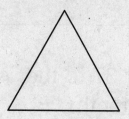

    A. Isosceles
    B. Right
    C. Scalene
    D. Equilateral

2. Estimate.

    4.72 + 5.14

    A. 8   **C.** 10
    B. 9   **D.** 11

3. Round 6.48 to the nearest whole number.

    A. 6   **C.** 64.8
    B. 6.5   **D.** 648

4. Five friends are standing in line at the fair: Ida, Noah, Jamila, Owen, and Pedro. Owen is third in line. Pedro is first in line. Noah is last in line. Ida is between Pedro and Owen. What is their order from front to back? Write the answer in a complete sentence.

_____

_____

_____

Give the length to the nearest $\frac{1}{2}$ in., $\frac{1}{4}$ in., and $\frac{1}{8}$ in.

5. |—————————————|

_____

6. Compare. Use <, >, or =.

    $\frac{3}{4} + \frac{5}{8}$ ◯ 1

Name_____

Spiral Review and Test Prep 11-7

Circle the correct answer.

1. Estimate $7.86 - 4.25$.

A. 2   **C.** 4

B. 3   **D.** 5

2. Add. You may use grids to help.

$6.57 + 1.3 =$

A. 6.87   **C.** 7.87

B. 6.97   **D.** 7.97

3. Which is the value of x in the equation $x - 4 = 10$?

A. $x = 6$ **C.** $x = 12$

B. $x = 8$ **D.** $x = 14$

4. Marlene's piano lesson began at 3:50 P.M. If it lasted for 35 min, at what time did the lesson end?

A. 4:15 P.M.

B. 4:25 P.M.

C. 4:35 P.M.

D. 4:45 P.M.

5. Draw the shape that comes next.

6. Add. Simplify if necessary.

$\frac{5}{9} + \frac{1}{9} =$

_____

7. Which is greater, 2 mi or 9,750 ft?

_____

8. Which is the shorter distance to walk, $\frac{1}{2}$ mi or 2,620 ft?

_____

Spiral Review and Test Prep 11-8

Circle the correct answer.

1. Subtract. You may use grids to help.

   $4.3 - 2.61 =$

   A. 1.49   **C.** 1.69
   B. 1.59   **D.** 1.79

2. Which is the sum of $0.92 + 13.59$?

   A. 14.51   **C.** 14.71
   B. 14.61   **D.** 14.81

3. Multiply.

   $\$0.79 \times 8 =$

   A. $6.92   **C.** $6.32
   B. $6.72   **D.** $6.12

4. Which is the product of $\$14.97 \times 6$?

   A. $89.62   **C.** $90.02
   B. $89.82   **D.** $90.22

Find each sum. Simplify, if necessary.

5. $\frac{4}{7} + \frac{6}{7} =$ _____

6. $\frac{4}{5} + \frac{4}{5} =$ _____

Tell whether an exact answer is needed or if an estimate is enough. Then solve.

7. CDs cost $12.95 each. If Jake has $30, does he have enough to buy 3 CDs?

   _____

8. Write a fact family for 7, 9, and 63.

   _____

   _____

   _____

Name_____

Spiral Review and Test Prep 11-9

Circle the correct answer.

1. Add.

$$\frac{5}{12} + \frac{5}{6} =$$

A. $1\frac{1}{2}$ **C.** $1\frac{1}{6}$

B. $1\frac{1}{4}$ **D.** $1\frac{1}{12}$

2. Subtract.

$$\frac{1}{3} - \frac{1}{4} =$$

A. $\frac{7}{12}$ **C.** $\frac{3}{12}$

B. $\frac{4}{12}$ **D.** $\frac{1}{12}$

3. Add.

$$41.67 + 8.52 =$$

A. 49.19 **C.** 50.19

B. 49.29 **D.** 50.29

4. Which is the product of 83 × 19?

A. 1,477 **C.** 1,677

B. 1,577 **D.** 1,777

5. There are 16 teams competing in the baseball tournament. A team is out of the tournament as soon as it loses 1 game. The winners of each round play again until there is just 1 champion. How many rounds will there be in the tournament?

_____

6. Ryan has 4 cats named Fluffy, Midnight, Mittens, and Tabby. One is orange, one black, one white, and one gray. Mittens is gray. Tabby is not white. Midnight is black. What color is Fluffy? Write the answer in a complete sentence.

_____

Spiral Review and Test Prep 11-10

Circle the correct answer.

1. Subtract.

$$\frac{9}{10} - \frac{3}{10}$$

A. $\frac{1}{2}$ **C.** $\frac{7}{10}$

B. $\frac{3}{5}$ **D.** $\frac{4}{5}$

2. Which is the sum of $\frac{7}{9} + \frac{1}{3}$?

A. $1\frac{1}{9}$ **C.** $1\frac{1}{3}$

B. $1\frac{1}{6}$ **D.** $1\frac{1}{2}$

3. If 12 books cost $24, how much do 5 books cost?

A. $5   **C.** $10

B. $8   **D.** $16

4. Which unit would you use to measure the width of a room?

A. Millimeter

B. Centimeter

C. Meter

D. Kilometer

Use the bar graph for 5–6.

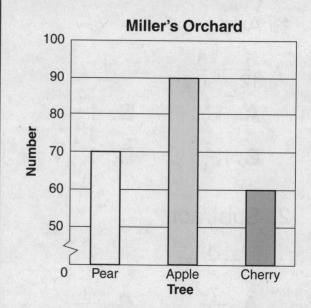

Miller's Orchard

5. How many cherry trees are in the orchard?

_____

6. How many more apple trees than pear trees are in the orchard?

_____

7. Mona has a 4 yd piece of rope to cut into three equal pieces. How long should each piece be?

_____

Spiral Review and Test Prep 11-11

Circle the correct answer.

1. Choose the most appropriate unit to use to measure the length of a grain of rice.

  A. Kilometer
  B. Millimeter
  C. Meter
  D. Decimeter

2. Choose the most appropriate unit to use to measure the capacity of a large bucket.

  A. Milliliter
  B. Kilometer
  C. Centimeter
  D. Liter

3. Subtract.

$$\frac{5}{6} - \frac{1}{12} =$$

  A. $\frac{1}{2}$ **C.** $\frac{2}{3}$

  B. $\frac{7}{12}$ **D.** $\frac{3}{4}$

4. What is the difference of $\frac{3}{4} - \frac{5}{8}$?

_____

5.

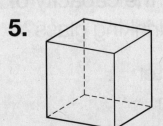

Identify the solid.

_____

6. Five friends are sitting on a bench: Opal, Jarvis, Nadia, Pilar, and Ira. Opal is in the middle. Nadia is on the far left. Pilar is on the far right. Ira is between Nadia and Opal. What is their order from left to right?

_____

_____

Spiral Review and Test Prep 11-12

Circle the correct answer.

1. Which is the most appropriate unit to use to measure the capacity of a small drinking glass?

   A. Milliliter
   B. Gram
   C. Liter
   D. Centimeter

2. Choose the most appropriate unit to use to measure the mass of a mouse.

   A. Meter   **C.** Liter
   B. Gram   **D.** Kilogram

3. Evaluate the expression $4n$ for $n = 5$.

   A. 8   **C.** 20
   B. 12   **D.** 26

4. Evaluate the expression $\frac{45}{k}$ for $k = 9$.

   A. 3   **C.** 5
   B. 4   **D.** 6

Add. Simplify, if necessary.

5. $\frac{4}{5} + \frac{3}{5} =$ _____

6. $\frac{7}{9} + \frac{8}{9} =$ _____

Tell whether an exact answer is needed or if an estimate is enough. Then solve.

7. Mrs. Haley is driving to her sister's house. In the morning, she drove 112 mi. Then she took a break and had lunch. In the afternoon, Mrs. Haley drove 89 mi. If her sister's house is 300 mi away, how much farther does Mrs. Haley have to drive?

_____

Find each product.

8. $\$3.45 \times 16 =$ _____

9. $\$5.61 \times 23 =$ _____

Name _____

Spiral Review and Test Prep 11-13

Circle the correct answer.

Add. Simplify, if necessary.

1. Divide.

$$\$6.72 \div 3 =$$

A. $2.04   **C.** $2.24
B. $2.09   **D.** $2.29

2. Which is the quotient of
$8.40 ÷ 5?

A. $1.54   **C.** $1.64
B. $1.58   **D.** $1.68

3. Choose the most
appropriate unit to use
to measure the mass of
an elephant.

A. Kilometer
B. Gram
C. Liter
D. Kilogram

4. Find the median.

36, 37, 39, 33, 34

A. 36   **C.** 38
B. 37   **D.** 39

5. $\frac{5}{6} + \frac{2}{3} =$ _____

6. $\frac{5}{8} + \frac{1}{4} =$ _____

7. Ryan has four pets
named Brandy, Bailey,
Jimmy, and Sparky.
One is a cat, one a fish,
one a bird, and one a
dog. Brandy is a dog.
Bailey is not a bird.
Sparky is a fish. What
kind of animal is
Jimmy? Write the
answer in a complete
sentence.

_____

Find the missing number.

8. 2,400 cm = _____ m

9. 17 kg = _____ g

Name_____

Spiral Review and Test Prep 11-14

Circle the correct answer.

1. Which is the product of
83 × 18?

  A. 1,394   **C.** 1,594
  B. 1,494   **D.** 1,694

2. Multiply.

  98 × 34 =

  A. 3,312   **C.** 3,332
  B. 3,322   **D.** 3,342

3. There are 4 boxes
marked with the letters
A, B, C, and D. A $100
bill, a toy, a balloon, and
a picture are in the
boxes. The balloon is
not in Box A or Box D.
The toy is in Box B. The
picture is in Box A. In
which box is the $100
bill?

  A. A   **C.** C
  B. B   **D.** D

4. Subtract.

$$\frac{3}{4} - \frac{2}{3} =$$

_____

Find the difference. Simplify,
if necessary.

5. $\frac{7}{8} - \frac{5}{8} =$ _____

6. $\frac{5}{7} - \frac{4}{7} =$ _____

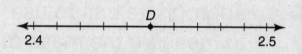

7. Explain how you know
the value of point D on
the number line.

_____

_____

_____

_____

8. 42 cm = _____ mm

Name_____

Spiral Review and Test Prep 11-15

Circle the correct answer.

1. Subtract.

$$\frac{10}{11} - \frac{4}{11} =$$

A. $\frac{3}{11}$ **C.** $\frac{5}{11}$

B. $\frac{4}{11}$ **D.** $\frac{6}{11}$

2. Which is the sum of
$\frac{13}{15} + \frac{4}{15}$?

A. $\frac{9}{15}$ **C.** $1\frac{2}{15}$

B. $\frac{3}{5}$ **D.** $1\frac{4}{15}$

3.

What is the temperature in °F?

A. 24°   **C.** 76°

B. 26°   **D.** 82°

4. Each bag contains 100 marbles. One of every 3 bags of marbles contains a silver marble. Predict about how many silver marbles there will be in 2,000 marbles. Explain how you made your prediction.

_____

_____

_____

_____

_____

_____

5. Ken bought a pen for $1.39, a notebook for $0.99, and a juice for $1.99 at the school bookstore. If Ken started with $10.00, how much does he have left?

_____

Spiral Review and Test Prep 12-1

Circle the correct answer.

1. Which is the temperature shown in °C?

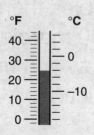

A. 25   **C.** −4
B. 21   **D.** −8

2. Which is twenty-nine and five-tenths in standard form?

A. 295   **C.** 2.95
B. 29.5   **D.** 0.295

3. Which is the sum of 2.46 + 16.9?

A. 19.16
B. 19.26
C. 19.36
D. 19.46

4. Jason saw 8 silver cars, 5 black cars, 4 blue cars, and 3 red cars. Predict about how many cars out of 138 will be blue. Explain.

_____

_____

_____

_____

5. Order the numbers from least to greatest.
6.7, 3.4, 9.3

_____

6. Each section of rope has a knot at each end. How many knots are needed to make 8 sections of rope?

_____

Spiral Review and Test Prep 12-2

Circle the correct answer.

1. Divide.

$61 \div 8 =$

A. 7 R2
B. 7 R3
C. 7 R4
D. 7 R5

2. Which is the correct graph of the inequality $a > 4$?

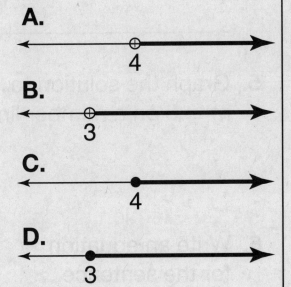

A.

4

B.

3

C.

4

D.

3

3. Round 26.82 to the nearest tenth.

A. 30   **C.** 26.8
B. 27   **D.** 26.0

4. Order the numbers from greatest to least.

4.54, 5.45, 4.45

_____

5. Hank has a 20 ft piece of wood he wants to have cut into 5 smaller pieces. The woodshop charges $4 for each cut. How much must Hank pay for the cuts?

_____

6. If the temperature outside is 12°C, would you go swimming? Explain why or why not.

_____

_____

_____

_____

_____

Spiral Review and Test Prep 12-3

Circle the correct answer.

1. Estimate.

$3.26 + 6.85$ **A.** 8

                  B. 9

                  C. 10

                  D. 11

2. Add.

      49   **A.** 257

      72   **B.** 267

  + 136   **C.** 277

                 D. 287

3. Round 7.53 to the nearest whole number.

A. 10   **C.** 7.5

B. 8   **D.** 7.6

4. The computers in a classroom are labeled with a number and a letter such as 2D. The numbers used are 1, 2, 3, and 4, and they are always listed before the letters. The letters used are A, B, C, D, and E. How many different number-letter combinations are possible?

_____

5. Graph the solution to $m \geq 8$ on a number line.

6. Write an equation for the sentence 4 times n is 20.

_____

Spiral Review and Test Prep 12-4

Circle the correct answer.

1. Choose the correct equation for the sentence. 4 fish plus x fish is 19.

   A. $4x = 19$
   B. $4 \div x = 19$
   C. $4 + x = 19$
   D. $4 - x = 19$

2. Add. You may use grids to help.

   $$\begin{array}{r} 8.7 \\ + 3.46 \\ \hline \end{array}$$

   A. 12.13
   B. 12.16
   C. 12.23
   D. 12.26

3. Find the value of y for $x = 3$.

   $y = 4x + 2$

   A. 12   C. 16
   B. 14   D. 18

4. Music class begins at 9:55 A.M. and ends at 10:40 A.M. How long is music class?

   _____

Find the sum or difference.

5. $$\begin{array}{r} 14.29 \\ + 6.5 \\ \hline \end{array}$$ _____

6. $$\begin{array}{r} 17.8 \\ - 3.92 \\ \hline \end{array}$$ _____

7. A school cafeteria prepares 4 tacos for every 3 students. How many tacos are prepared for 30 students? Write the answer in a complete sentence.

   _____

   _____

   _____

Spiral Review and Test Prep 12-5

Circle the correct answer.

1. Subtract. You may use grids to help.

$$\begin{array}{r} 7.81 \\ -\ 4.9\ \ \\ \hline \end{array}$$

 A. 2.81
 B. 2.89
 C. 2.91
 D. 2.99

2. Which is the sum of 1.04 + 26.78?

 A. 27.52   **C.** 27.72
 B. 27.62   **D.** 27.82

3. Beth has enough ribbon to decorate 4 packages. Each package takes 4 pieces of ribbon. How many ribbon cuts will she have to make?

 A. 10   **C.** 15
 B. 12   **D.** 18

4. Multiply. $12.86 × 7

 A. $90.02   **C.** $90.22
 B. $90.12   **D.** $90.32

5. Graph the equation $y = x + 3$.

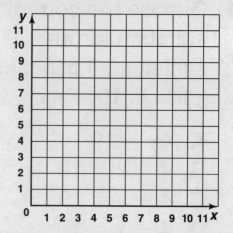

Decide if the problem has extra information or missing information. Solve if you have enough information.

6.

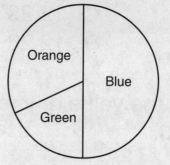

Favorite colors

How many students chose blue as their favorite color?

_____

Spiral Review and Test Prep 12-6

Circle the correct answer.

1. There are 8 players in the tennis tournament. Each player plays every other player once. How many tennis matches will there be?

A. 56   **C.** 28

B. 38   **D.** 26

2. $\frac{5}{8} + \frac{1}{2} =$

A. $\frac{3}{4}$ **C.** $1\frac{1}{8}$

B. $\frac{7}{8}$ **D.** $1\frac{1}{4}$

3. Add.

$$\begin{array}{r} 52.84 \\ + 13.75 \\ \hline \end{array}$$

A. 66.49
B. 66.59
C. 66.69
D. 66.79

4. Which object's mass would be measured using kilograms?

A. Pen   **C.** Ice cube

B. Eraser   **D.** Snow plow

Decide if the problem has extra or missing information. Solve if you have enough information.

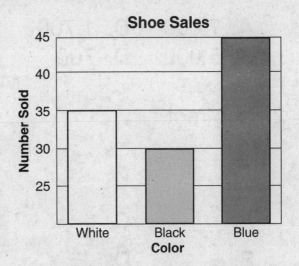

Shoe Sales

5. Randa bought a pair of white shoes. Emily bought a pair of blue shoes. How many more pairs of blue shoes were sold than white shoes?

_____

6. A bag has only two red chips. Tell whether it is likely, unlikely, impossible, or certain to pick a red chip.

_____

Spiral Review and Test Prep 12-7

Circle the correct answer.

1. How many meters are equal to 7 km?

   A. 7,000   **C.** 1,700

   B. 5,000   **D.** 700

2. Subtract.

$$\frac{9}{10} - \frac{4}{10} =$$

   A. $\frac{2}{5}$ **C.** $\frac{3}{5}$

   B. $\frac{1}{2}$ **D.** $\frac{7}{10}$

3. A carton of 6 eggs costs $0.48. How much do 2 eggs cost?

   A. $0.08   **C.** $0.24

   B. $0.16   **D.** $0.32

4. What is the most appropriate unit to measure the distance between two cities?

   A. Millimeter

   B. Centimeter

   C. Meter

   D. Kilometer

5. Tell whether it is likely, unlikely, impossible, or certain for the spinner to land on C.

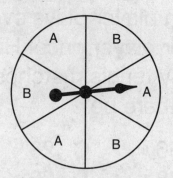

_____

6. List all of the possible outcomes for spinning both spinners below at the same time.

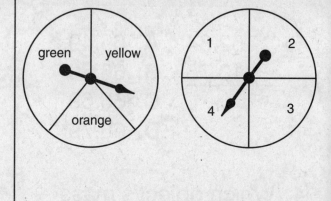

_____

_____

_____

Spiral Review and Test Prep 12-8

Circle the correct answer.

1. Choose the most appropriate unit to measure the length of a swimming pool.

A. Milliliter   **C.** Meter
B. Millimeter   **D.** Liter

2. Choose the most appropriate unit to measure the capacity of a spoon.

A. Milliliter   **C.** Meter
B. Millimeter   **D.** Liter

3.

What is the probability the spinner will land on 2?

A. $\frac{3}{3}$ **C.** $\frac{1}{8}$

B. $\frac{3}{8}$ **D.** $\frac{4}{8}$

4. List all of the possible outcomes for spinning the spinner and tossing the number cube with numbers 1 through 6.

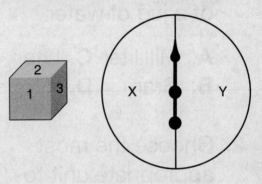

_____

_____

_____

_____

5. Walter bought a 6 ft long sandwich for the party. Nine people are at the party. How many cuts in the sandwich must Walter make for everyone to get an equal-sized portion?

_____

Name_____

Spiral Review and Test Prep 12-9

Circle the correct answer.

1. Choose the most appropriate unit to measure the capacity of a jug of water.

    A. Milliliter **C.** Liter
    B. Gram   **D.** Kilogram

2. Choose the most appropriate unit to measure the mass of a boat.

    A. Milliliter **C.** Liter
    B. Gram   **D.** Kilogram

3. A spinner has four equal-sized sections labeled red, blue, green, and yellow. What is the probability the spinner will land on green?

    A. $\frac{4}{4}$ **C.** $\frac{2}{4}$

    B. $\frac{3}{4}$ **D.** $\frac{1}{4}$

4. How many times would you expect a coin to land tails up when it is flipped 50 times?

_____

5. Marcus has 11 marbles. Three of them are gold, 5 are orange, 2 are green, and 1 is blue. Explain how to predict about how many out of 100 marbles will be green.

_____

_____

_____

_____

_____

_____

Find the product.

6. $6.72
    $\times$ 34
    _____

Spiral Review and Test Prep 12-10

Circle the correct answer.

1. How many centimeters are equal to 40 m?

   A. 40,000 **C.** 400
   B. 4,000   **D.** 4

2. School starts at 8:15 A.M. Becca has a 10 min walk to the bus stop and a 20 min bus ride to school. What time should she leave her house to get to school on time?

   A. 7:45 A.M.
   B. 7:50 A.M.
   C. 7:55 A.M.
   D. 8:00 A.M.

3. Choose the most appropriate unit for measuring the mass of a shoe.

   A. Centimeter
   B. Gram
   C. Meter
   D. Kilogram

4.

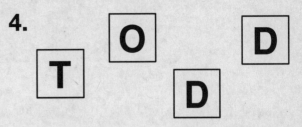

Predict how many times you would pick the letter D if you picked a letter 20 times, putting the letter back after each pick.

_____

5. There are 16 teams in the soccer tournament. A team is out of the tournament if it loses a game. The winners of each round play again until there is just one champion. How many soccer games will be played in the tournament?

_____